Scripture Discussion Commentary 2

SCRIPTURE DISCUSSION COMMENTARY 2

Series editor: Laurence Bright

Prophets I

Amos and Hosea *Ann Macpherson*
Isaiah 1-39 *Joseph Rhymer*
Jeremiah *John Challenor*
Isaiah 40-66 *John Challenor*

ACTA Foundation
Adult Catechetical Teaching Aids
Chicago, Illinois

First published 1971
ACTA Foundation (Adult Catechetical Teaching Aids),
4848 N. Clark Street, Chicago, Illinois 60640
© 1971 Ann Macpherson, Joseph Rhymer, John Challenor
Nihil obstat : John M. T. Barton STD LSS *Censor*
Imprimatur : + Victor Guazzelli *Vicar General*
Westminster, 9th July 1971

2539

Library of Congress number 71–173033
ISBN 0 87946 001 6
Made and printed in Great Britain by
William Clowes & Sons, Limited
London, Beccles and Colchester

Contents

Jeremiah   *John Challenor*

General Introduction

A few of the individual units which make up this series of biblical commentaries have already proved their worth issued as separate booklets. Together with many others they are now grouped together in a set of twelve volumes covering almost all the books of the old and new testaments—a few have been omitted as unsuitable to the general purpose of the series.

That purpose is primarily to promote discussion. This is how these commentaries differ from the others that exist. They do not cover all that could be said about the biblical text, but concentrate on the features most likely to get lively conversation going—those, for instance, with special relevance for later developments of thought, or for life in the church and world of today. For this reason passages of narrative are punctuated by sets of questions designed to get a group talking, though the text of scripture, helped by the remarks of the commentator, should have already done just that.

For the text is what matters. Individuals getting ready for a meeting, the group itself as it meets, should always have the bible centrally present, and use the commentary only as a tool. The bibliographies will help those wishing to dig deeper.

What kinds of group can work in this way? Absolutely

any. The bible has the reputation of being difficult, and in some respects it is, but practice quickly clears up a lot of initial obstacles. So parish groups of any kind can and should be working on it. The groups needn't necessarily already exist, it is enough to have a few like-minded friends and to care sufficiently about finding out what the bible means. Nor need they be very large; one family could be quite enough. High schools (particularly in the senior year), colleges and universities are also obvious places for groups to form. If possible they should everywhere be ecumenical in composition: though all the authors are Roman catholics, there is nothing sectarian in their approach.

In each volume there are two to four, or occasionally more, studies of related biblical books. Each one is self-contained; it is neither necessary nor desirable to start at the beginning and plough steadily through. Take up, each time, what most interests you—there is very little in scripture that is actually dull! Since the commentaries are by different authors, you will discover differences of outlook, in itself a matter for discussion. Above all, remember that getting the right general approach to reading the bible is more important than answering any particular question about the text—and that this approach only comes with practice.

LAURENCE BRIGHT

Amos and Hosea

Ann Macpherson

Introduction

Amos and Hosea were both active as prophets during the period preceding the defeat and exile of the inhabitants of Israel, the northern kingdom, by Assyria. Both prophets interpreted these events as God's punishment on Israel for her sin. Israel had emerged as a separate state only after the death of Solomon, although there had been a brief separation of Israel and Judah at the death of Saul. The reign of Solomon had been in many ways 'the golden age'. After his death the northern kingdom had rebelled against the Davidic dynasty and had chosen Jeroboam i as the leader of a separate state. Under the dynasty of Jehu Israel enjoyed political acclaim and material prosperity. By the time of Amos and Hosea there had been a severe moral and spiritual decline. Affluence had made the people greedy for even more money and more luxuries. Not all the Israelites shared in this prosperity however. From Amos we learn of the existence of a class which was both bitterly poor and savagely exploited. Israelite religion too was in decline and had become contaminated by the practices of Canaanite paganism. It was not that the Israelites had stopped worshipping Yahweh but that they had tried to combine this worship with the worship of Baalim, the gods of Canaan.

The message of Amos was directed against the social

injustices of his time. Outward religious ceremony was of no value or meaning unless it was accompanied by concern for the welfare of others; God wanted sincerity, not empty gestures of sacrifice and obedience. This teaching of Amos is surely no less relevant to us today, living as we do in a world where more than half the inhabitants go hungry and where individuals and whole nations are constantly exploited. We might also recall the words of St John's first epistle: 'We love because he first loved us. If anyone says "I love God" and hates his brother, he is a liar; for he who does not love his brother whom he has seen, cannot love God whom he has not seen. And this commandment we have from him, that he who loves God should love his brother also' (1 Jn 4:19–21).

Although he shared Amos' concern with social justice, Hosea's central theme was the love relationship between Yahweh and his bride, Israel. This covenant relationship had existed since God first chose Israel, but Israel, like an unfaithful wife, has betrayed his love and his trust. This image of Israel as Yahweh's bride is used by several of the old testament prophets to bring home to God's people the full meaning of their relationship with him. In the new testament, and especially in Ephesians chapter 5, the same image is applied to the relationship between Christ and the church.

Book list

J. Rhymer, *The Prophets & the Law* (Sheed and Ward).
G. Von Rad, *The Message of the Prophets* (SCM Press).
John Marsh, *Amos and Micah* (SCM Press).
G. Knight, *Hosea* (SCM Press).

1

Oracles against Israel and the nations
Amos 1:1–3:8

Amos 1:1–2

These two opening verses really form the title for the book. It is unlikely that Amos was the author of the complete work. In all probability a later editor supplied the additional introductory background to this collection of prophetic utterances. Two main points are made concerning the person of Amos and his date. Amos is introduced as one of the shepherds of Tekoa (modern Tequ'a), hill country lying about six miles south of Bethlehem. It has been suggested that the actual Hebrew word for shepherd used here means a person who raises a special breed of sheep famous for their high quality wool. If this was true then Amos was probably not a poor shepherd. The word is also used in reference to the king of Moab, 2 Kgs 3:4. Amos is recorded as proclaiming God's message when Uzziah was king of Judah (781–740) and Jeroboam II ruled in Israel (783–743): that is somewhere between 780–740 BC. An earthquake is mentioned but although this may have been a useful reference for very early readers of Amos it does not help us, as the exact date of the event is unknown. The internal evidence, however, suggests a date late in the reign of Jeroboam II; in particular the awareness of danger from Assyria which only materialised after the rise of Tiglath-pileser III (745–727).

Amos' message is for Israel, the northern kingdom; the tone is conveyed by the sentence 'the Lord roars from Zion'—a picture of a ravaging lion seeking its prey. The severity of the punishment is indicated in the latter half of the verse. Drought will cause even fertile areas like Carmel to wither and the pastures will be thoroughly scorched.

Amos 1:3–2:5. Sayings against the nations

This section consists of a series of six condemnations all following a similar pattern. The expression at the beginning of each oracle . . . 'for three transgressions of . . . and for four' indicates an indefinite but excessive number.

First in the series is *Damascus*, the capital of Syria and frequently in violent conflict with Israel. Threshing irons metaphorically illustrate her cruelty towards the Gileadites (see 2 Kgs 10:32–33). King Hazael (842–806) and his son Benhadad III were two of the latest kings to make Israel suffer. So much for the crimes of Damascus; her punishment will be destruction by war. The 'bar' is a reference to the city gate. It is possible that the valley of Aven (*wickedness*, possibly Baalbek or the plain of Damascus) and Betheden are symbolic names for Damascus, which fell to the Assyrians in 732 BC and the Syrians were exiled, 2 Kgs 16:9.

Four of the five Philistine city states which were established from 1200 BC are mentioned in the next oracle (1:6–8). Gaza is charged with selling a whole tribe into slavery to Edom. Slave traffic was rife in the ancient Near East. (No specific charge is held against

Ashdod, Ashkelon or Ekron). Their punishment was to be the destruction of the city states *and* the obliteration of the Philistines (1:9–10). Tyre, the kingdom of the Phoenicians, was also to suffer devastation for slave trade. The covenant of brotherhood mentioned in 1:9 is possibly a reference to a treaty made between Solomon and Hiram king of Tyre. There had also been a marriage tie between Ahab of Israel and Jezebel, daughter of the Phoenician king, 1 Kgs 16:31. Israel, the northern kingdom, and Tyre had also on occasions united against Damascus.

The next oracle (1:11 and 12) charged Edom with the persecution of Israel and with brutality in war. There was a brother relationship between Israel and Edom on account of their ancestors Jacob and Esau (Gen 25:22–27:40) but the Edomites apparently ignored this. Again the punishment is destruction. The name Teman refers to a district, clan or city of Edom. Bozrah was an important city which can most probably be identified with the modern el-Busaireh, twenty miles south-east of the Dead Sea.

Ammon's greed for land led to crimes of brutality (1:13–15) and for this the Ammonites would be exiled. Rabbah was the chief Ammonite city. The 'shouting' mentioned in 1:14 probably refers to the war-cries of Arab tribes. The Ammonite rulers were responsible; they would go into exile.

The first oracle of the second chapter deals with the Moabites (2:1–3), the descendants of Lot by his two daughters (Gen 19:27–38). This tribe is to be punished for cremating a royal corpse. Nothing more is known of this act, which went against the Semitic idea that undisturbed burial was necessary for the peace of the departed. It is interesting to note that this was not a crime against Israel but against Edom, Israel's enemy.

Perhaps this oracle is an indication of the realisation that Yahweh's standard is universal and his justice applicable to all nations. Kerioth (2:2) is possibly twentieth-century Kerak; according to the Moabite stone it was the chief city of Moab, and the home of Chemosh, the Moabite god.

Now the prophet appears to turn to Judah, the kingdom of the south (2:4–5). Her crime is her rejection of Yahweh's law. The authenticity of this passage has been questioned and the suggestion has been made that it is a later interpolation inserted to turn Amos' message to Judah. Some supporters of this idea maintain that for Amos the term 'Israel' included both kingdoms.

What parallels are there between the crimes of these cities and the behaviour of states or power blocs today?

Amos 2:6–16. Oracles against Israel

The list of crimes brought in the charge against Israel is more developed and detailed than those against the nations. Israel's crimes are contrasted with Yahweh's generosity towards her. Her crimes include 'selling the righteous for silver and the needy for a pair of shoes', (2:6) a reference to the slave trade or the practice of bribing judges to condemn an innocent man; the second phrase probably rests on some symbolic action used in the legal transfer of property. The poor man is swindled but the dealing is made to look legal. The first part of 2:7 gives a hyperbolic description of the exploitation of the poor by the rich: the second half of the verse is probably a reference to sacred prostitution, or to some form of the fertility cult. 'Garments taken in pledge' (2:8) is a reference to the giving of a garment to a creditor as security. According to Deut 24:12 this garment had to be returned at dusk but in Amos 2:8 it seems to be used in idolatrous worship. The verse ends with a reference to the sacred banquets or orgies associated with sacrifice. Yahweh is not honoured by such acts, hence the use of the expression 'their God'. This kind of religious practice rested on the exploitation of the poor.

Amos then recalls what God has done for Israel (2:9–12). He destroyed the Canaanites, brought them from Egypt, yet Israel is not grateful; she rejected the prophets and tried to make the Nazirites break their abstention from wine. Her doom is portrayed in 2:13–16. Israel will be crushed relentlessly, there will be no escape, not even for the swift and mighty.

Can any fruitful comparison be made between the sins of Israel enumerated by Amos and the sins of christians living in the developed countries of the world today?

Amos 3:1–9

In chapter 3 Amos calls Israel, both kingdoms, 'the whole family which I brought up out of the land of Egypt to hear Yahweh's word; and Yahweh's word is a threat of punishment'. The authority and origin of Amos' message is dealt with in 3:3–8, arguing on the lines of cause and effect. If Yahweh speaks Amos can do nothing else but prophesy. A prophet speaks because God has inspired him; and when God inspires him he cannot but speak. Throughout the passage Yahweh is likened to a lion about to pounce on Israel, his prey. It is reminiscent of one of the opening verses: 'The Lord roars from Sion . . .' (1:2). The trap or snare which Yahweh has set for Israel is inescapable (3:5). Trumpets (3:6) were used to signal danger.

Does evil befall a city unless the Lord has done it? (3:6) In these verses and throughout the book Amos makes no distinction between what God permits and what he directly causes, nor between primary and secondary causes. Whatever happens it is all due to Yahweh.

1. To what extent is it credible for us today to interpret political events and military defeats as punishments from God? 2. What is the role of the prophet in the church today?

2

Injustice and hypocrisy
Amos 3:9–4:13

Amos 3:9–4:5

Doom on Samaria is the theme of 3:9–12. The surrounding nations, Egypt and Assyria, are called to see the chaos
in Samaria. The people of Samaria no longer know right
from wrong; they get rich by robbery and violence. Her
punishment is destruction. The adversary (3:11) was
unnamed in Amos' day but Assyria provided the greatest
threat. On the day of Samaria's doom her inhabitants
will be so bewildered and afraid that they will not be
able to defend themselves. The Israelites who lived in
Samaria will be rescuing scraps of furniture from the
debris as the shepherd attempts to retrieve fragments
of the sheep's carcase from the lion's mouth, especially
those bearing lion's teeth marks so that he would not have
to make good the sheep.

The next passage calls someone, perhaps Assyria and
Egypt again, to hear and testify against the house of
Jacob. The contents of the following verses, however,
seem to apply to the northern kingdom. Bethel was a
patriarchal shrine which was given a new lease of life
when Jeroboam I set up the golden calf there so that the
inhabitants of the new northern kingdom need not go to
Jerusalem to worship. Amos attacks the cult on grounds
of insincerity; it was meaningless if Israel did not

maintain her moral obligations. The 'horns of the altar' (3:14) were horn-shaped projections on each of the corners. During sacrifices the victims' blood was smeared on them (Ex 27:2; 29:12). It was possible to claim asylum by grasping them (1 Kgs 1:50; 2:28). If they were struck off there could be no asylum; it would signify the end of the altar's power and imply that there was no escape from the punishment that loomed large. The Israelites' fine houses would also be destroyed. Excavations at Samaria have revealed ivory panelling and inlaid furniture. The wide gap between the standard of living of the rich and poor was not in keeping with a nation who had a covenant relationship with the living Yahweh.

Amos criticises the rich women of Samaria, calling them 'cows of Bashan'. 'Bashan' (4:1) was a fertile district across the river Jordan which was famous for its well-fed herds and flock. These indolent females, who were apparently fed and clothed at the expense of the poor, persuaded their husbands to bring them exotic drinks and other luxuries without regard for the needs of those they were exploiting. The prophet continues by proclaiming that 'God has sworn by his holiness' (4:2) that they will be punished. God is described as swearing by 'his holiness', meaning by himself, because there is no more potent name to use in an oath. Amos' description of their punishment and in particular his use of the word 'hook' (4:2) presents us with a number of equally powerful images; the victims are dragged away from their rich homes like fish being hauled out of water; like captives of the Assyrians being dragged along by hooks in the noses; like corpses being dragged to the refuse heap or, returning to the metaphor at the beginning of the chapter, as cattle being led by a hook in the muzzle. The women will be dragged out to the breaches in the city wall, probably a reference to the fall of Samaria which was to take place in 721 BC, and cast out into 'Harmon' (4:3). 'Harmon' is unknown, though the Jerusalem Bible renders this phrase 'towards Hermon' which was on the road to Assyria.

Amos goes on in a strongly sarcastic vein to condemn the hypocritical worship of the inhabitants of the northern kingdom at their ancient shrines, Bethel and Gilgal. Abraham had offered sacrifice at Bethel (Gen 12:8), though it was not known to him by that name, but this sanctuary was recharged when Jeroboam I (931–910) set up the golden calf as a symbol of the throne of Yahweh, making Bethel a major sanctuary for the northern kingdom. 'Gilgal' means a circle of stones; there were several places so named but this particular one was probably located near Jericho. The prophet is contrasting their very accurate, even excessive observance of the ritual or cultic law with the neglect of justice and love, cf 4:13. Perhaps the Israelites thought that God would not notice their evil way of life as long as they remained faithful to the laws of the cult. The transgression at Bethel and Gilgal was insincerity and religious formalism. The details of the sacrifices mentioned can be found in the law; for example, morning offerings in Num 28:23 and three-yearly tithes in Deut 26:12. Amos mentions tithes being paid 'every three days' (4:4; a likely explanation of this is sarcasm directed at the frequency of the ritual acts. The exhortation to 'publish' and 'proclaim' (4:5) freewill offerings refers to an injunction in Deut 12:18 that the offerer's household and the local levites should be invited to the sacred banquet which followed this particular sacrifice. There is a hint here that the worshippers at Bethel and Gilgal were more interested in the feast than the sacrifice and that what was originally prescribed for worship of Yahweh had become an occasion for ostentatious pleasure.

1. Is Amos' condemnation of the exploitation of the poor by the rich women of Samaria applicable in any way today; for example, how far is the exploitation of others an integral part of our economic system: is this avoidable?

2. Is the Roman catholic church any less prone than the Israelites of Amos' time to the danger of making ritual observance an end in itself?

3. What relevance does the passage studied have to our responsibility to the under-developed countries of the Third World?

Amos 4:6–13

God tried to teach Israel. The passage portrays God using natural disasters to persuade Israel to return to him. 'Cleanness of teeth' and 'lack of bread' refer to famine, which was all too common in Palestine. Drought three months before harvest was common. The harvest was in May; winter rain often ended early thus destroying the crop which was growing. Apparently the drought was less common; one city suffered but another did not, but the reserve of water in each city was not enough to supply strangers. The blight and mildew of 4:9 were due to scorching of the crops by the sirocco, a searing hot desert wind. Locusts too were a common pest. The Israelites suffered plagues like those brought upon the Egyptians; their camp smelt of corpses and still they did not repent. A literary parallel with the destruction of Sodom and Gomorrah was perhaps inevitable. 'The land plucked from the fire' seems to refer to some disaster from which the Israelites were snatched at the last moment.

Amos urges the Israelites again to repent, to prepare to meet Yahweh.

The doxology of 4:13–15 does not bear Amos' style; it is more like the writings of Deutero-Isaiah. It could have been inserted by a later editor. There are two more similar passages (5:8–9; 9:5–6). The theme of this particular doxology is that the forces of nature reveal God's glory and his transcendence.

What problems arise for us today when we attribute natural catastrophes to God's activity? Is such an attribution compatible either with a scientific view of the world or a christian understanding of God's love?

3
Woe to injustice
Amos 5:1–6:14

Amos 5:1–6. Lamentation on the fall of Israel

Israel's disasters are related as if they were already history. As in Hosea, Isaiah and Jeremiah, Israel is represented as a virgin. Israel's punishment takes the form of an invasion whose outcome is exile for the Israelites. Following this brief lamentation is an exhortation to 'seek Yahweh and live' (4–6). This is a call to genuine repentance. Sacrifice is not enough; the Lord says 'Seek me and live; but do not seek Bethel . . .'. The Israelites must desire to establish a living relationship with Yahweh and not the worship of the shrines. Beersheba was in the south of Judah, about fifty miles south-south-west of Jerusalem. Joseph was the ancestor of the tribes of Ephraim and Manasseh.

Amos 5:7 and 10–17

Verse 7 seems to be misplaced; most commentators agree that the text reads better if this verse follows 5:9. The doxology of 5:8–9 is probably an interpolation. It seems to interrupt Amos' thought-flow. The theme of this doxology is that the entire universe including the stars is directly controlled by Yahweh.

Amos condemns the judges who are unjust. For the poor

the law-courts should be a source of help and not of exploitation and oppression. Wormwood was a bitter plant used here to symbolise utter distaste. There was a public square just inside the city gates where disputes were heard and settled by the judge or the elders of the city. If any elder did uphold right behaviour he was hated by the others (5:10). The wheat levies mentioned in 5:11 also appeared to be an occasion for exploiting the poor. The wealthy landlords took more than their share from the poor who farmed their land; this practice directly contravened the law (Deut 23:19). The rich also had houses of hewn stone, like palaces, while the poor had to build their homes from any old stones found in the fields. When God's punishment came none of these fine houses would remain standing.

From 5:12 and 5:13 we learn that the council of elders who were responsible for the administration of justice in the city or village were corrupt. They took bribes to acquit the guilty; this was forbidden in Ex 21:20. The needy were turned away; they had no money so they received no hearing. The wise man did not bring his case to court for he knew he would not get a fair hearing. Then again the Israelites are exhorted to seek good and not evil that they may live. The life offered is not just physical existence but a relationship with Yahweh. Justice must be re-established in the courts. The 'remnant of Joseph' are the few who will remain after God's judgement. This judgement will be an occasion for mourning (16–17). Elaborate displays of grief were common in the Near East; there were professional wailers who could be hired for such an occasion; cf the death of Jairus' daughter in the new testament. The farmers are to be called to mourning and there will be wailing in the vineyards; normally the harvesting of the vines was an

occasion for rejoicing, but not this time, 'for I will pass
through the midst of you, says the Lord' calling to
mind the time when he passed through Egypt smiting the
Egyptian first-born.

*The denial of justice to the economically under-privileged has
been a common evil in every age. How does Amos' denunciation of
it apply*
    (*a*) *to us as more or less prejudiced individuals?*
    (*b*) *to justice in our own country?*
    (*c*) *to justice in the church?*

Amos 5:18–6:7. Three woes

Woe to those who wait for the day of the Lord. This day
would be, according to popular thought, a day of
national rejoicing, a day to be looked forward to. But
Amos claims that on the contrary it will be a day of
judgement, a black day for Israel. We find the same
theme in Hosea.

The prophet then returns to his condemnation of
meaningless religious ritual; meaningless because it was
insincere. Without justice the sacrificial worship is
hypocrisy. Yahweh does not want sacrifice but justice.

But let justice roll down like waters, and righteousness
like an ever flowing stream

The time spent by the Israelites in the wilderness after
the exodus was regarded by some prophets, including
Amos and Hosea (2:16), as Israel's honeymoon with
Yahweh; a time when the relationship was perfect.
According to some scholars the Israelites did not begin to
offer sacrifice to Yahweh until they began to live in the
land of Canaan, in spite of the many references to
sacrifice throughout the Pentateuch. But the point Amos

is making is surely that Israel's worship of Yahweh in the desert was simple and sincere. Sakkuth (26) is the name of an Assyrian-Babylonian god; Kaiwan is the Akkadian name for Saturn. These pagan idols could not save the Israelites, who would be taken into exile beyond Damascus, in other words, to Assyria.

Amos 6:1–8

Woe to the luxury-loving, rich rulers of both Judah and Israel; they shall all be punished by exile. Calneh (738 BC), Hamath (720 BC) and Gath in Philistia (711 BC) were all overcome by the Assyrians. Israel is to share the same fate.

Amos 6:4–7

Woe also to the indolent rich; those who lie on beds of ivory eating and drinking all day. The calves from the stall (6:4) were those that had been fed on milk only and were therefore very tender. They chose the fattest of the flock; they anointed themselves with the choicest oils (anointing was a common hygienic custom which offered some protection against the heat). They were over-indulgent, they took the best of everything and were so preoccupied with their own enjoyment that they did not give a thought to the threatened ruin of Israel. They would be the first to go into exile.

Amos 6:8–14. Yahweh makes an oath

Yahweh hates the materialistic arrogance of Judah; her palaces and cities would be destroyed. A description of a plague follows in 6:9–10. Plagues often followed sieges presumably because of the unburied corpses. Burying the dead was universal among the Hebrews; obviously this is an exception. It could conceivably be a reference not to burning the body but burning spices in honour of the dead. 'We must not mention the name of the Lord' (6:10); this sentiment could be based on superstitious fear of another outburst of God's anger or an expression of utter hopelessness that prayer will not do any good.

An earthquake will destroy the great house and the little house (6:11). Israel has done what is unreasonable; she has turned justice into bitterness. Lodebar (6:13) was a small town on the borders of Gad which might possibly be identified with the modern Ummed Debar; Karnaim, meaning 'horns' and therefore 'strength', was an ancient town in eastern Bashan; both had been re-captured from Damascus. The nation that Yahweh is raising up against the house of Israel is Assyria. The Assyrian will attack the Israelites from Hamath, a town in the Lebanon valley marking the northern limit of Israel's territory, to the brook of the Arabah; possibly a wadi which extends from the southern tip of the Dead Sea to the Gulf of Arabah. This marked the extent of the territory won by Jeroboam II (2 Kgs 14:20).

Why, as in 6:10, does superstition so often flourish in the absence of genuine religious commitment?

4

The visions of Amos
Amos 7:1–9:18

Amos 7:1–9:4. Amos' first three visions

It is quite possible that the visions related in these verses were originally Amos' call to prophesy. Each vision, except the fifth (9:1) is introduced by the formula 'Thus the Lord showed me'.

The subject of the first vision (7:1–3), a plague of locusts, was common enough in Palestine, perhaps actual experience underlies the vision. 'Grass' in this context means vegetation. God was forming locusts, that is he was directly responsible for their effect, 'in the beginning of the shooting up of the latter growth' ie while the second crop was growing. The first crop often went to the king as tax. The first crop was sown before the middle of January and the second between the middle of January and the end of February. So the locusts which Yahweh was in the process of forming would destroy both crops. Amos is represented as interceding for Israel; this intervention makes Yahweh, the God of love and mercy, relent and the promised doom is withheld. Elsewhere in the book of Amos (4:9) the actual sending of a plague of locusts by God to warn Israel to mend her ways was seen as an act of mercy.

The second vision (7:4–10) pictured God preparing judgement by fire. This fire devoured the great deep or

the abyss which represented for the Hebrews the sub-
terranean waters on which they thought the earth floated
and which was thought to be the source of rivers and
floods. The fire was also burning up the land, thus this
great fire would deprive the people of food and water.
Amos pleads again, this time on account of Israel's
smallness and weakness. Again the prophet's intervention is successful.

The third vision (7:7–9) was that of the plumbline. A
plumbline was used for testing; Israel was tested by
Yahweh and found wanting, she was like a bulging wall.
She was not true because she had abused the covenant
relationship with Yahweh. This time Amos does not
intervene. God's judgement on Israel is irrevocable and
consists of destruction by invasion. The concluding verse
of this vision, 'and I will rise against the house of
Jeroboam with the sword' is a probable reference to the
murder, in 743 BC, of Zechariah, son of Jeroboam II; it
also provides a link with the historical interlude which
follows (7:10–17).

*Can we still think of intercessory prayer in terms of changing
God's decisions? If prayer does not alter events what reasons are
there for praying for others at all?*

Amos 7:10–17. Conflict with the establishment

In this passage we feel the friction between the prophet
and priest; between Amos, the revolutionary who wanted
to change social standards, and the establishment
symbolised by Amaziah, the king's priest. Amaziah was
the chief priest at Bethel, the king's sanctuary and the
official shrine of the northern kingdom. Amaziah distor-
ted the words of Amos and accused him of conspiracy
against Jeroboam. His command to Amos to go to

Judah and prophesy there implies that Amaziah had mistaken Amos for one of the many professional seers who served at the local shrines, pandering to pagan practices and only interested in money. Amos denied any connection with these professional prophets and described himself as a 'dresser of sycamore trees'. The fruit of the sycamore was food for the poor; it was like the fig but smaller and it needed to be punctured at a particular time by a dresser so that it could grow big enough to be edible. From the beginning of the book we know that Amos was also a shepherd. Amos declared that he prophesied solely because God had said 'Go prophesy to my people in Israel'. The encounter with Amaziah ends with Amos' description of the impending invasion and its accompanying horrors, rape, plunder, innocent deaths and exile. The land of exile (7:17) is Assyria, which is labelled unclean because of the idolatrous practices of the Assyrian people.

Do prophets inevitably come into conflict with the representatives of institutional religion? Suggest some other examples from more recent times.

Amos 8:1–3. The fourth vision

This vision of a basket of summer fruit suggests that the time is ripe for judgement. There is a play on the words 'summer fruit' and 'end' in the Hebrew text. God will not pardon Israel, the end has come.

Amos 8:4–14. Condemnation of the rich and greedy

The rich landlords and others who exploited and oppressed the poor were apparently impatient to see the end of a holy day or festival so that they could return to their profitable efforts. According to Num 28:11–15 the

2—P. I.

first day of each new lunar month was celebrated with a sacrifice; and like the sabbath it was a day of rest. An 'ephah' was a dry measure of a little more than a bushel. The Jewish law forbade merchants to use dishonest ephah measures (Lev 19:36, Deut 25:14–15). A shekel was a unit of weight; stones were used for weights. Dishonest traders fiddled the balance. The 'refuse of wheat' was that which should have been discarded; a possible interpretation is that the merchants were so greedy they sold even this.

The next passage returns to the subject of Israel's punishment (8:7) 'The pride of Jacob' is possibly a synonym for Yahweh himself since it would be unfitting for him to swear by anything other than himself. Verse 8 describes an earthquake in terms of the flooding of Egypt by the Nile. An eclipse (8:9) was a sign of doom. There was a total eclipse of the sun by the moon in June 763 in Palestine. The Israelite feasts were to be turned into days of mourning. 'Sackcloth' and 'shaven heads' were signs of sorrow. Another famine is promised (11–12), a famine of God's words. The Israelites will search in vain for a prophet, even though they wander from sea to sea, possibly from the Mediterranean to the Euphrates. The punishment for idolatry falls on the young as well as the old leaving no hope for the future. Verse 14 is a brief condemnation of syncretism. Dan and Beersheba were the extreme northern and southern limits of the country and were both centres of idolatrous worship. Dan with Bethel had been raised to the status of a national shrine by Jeroboam I. At these shrines Yahweh was worshipped together with pagan gods such as Ashimah.

Now read Mt 6:24. How easy is it for human beings to combine religious observance with materialistic values?

Amos 9:1–6. The fifth vision

A most likely setting for this final vision is the sanctuary at Bethel where the Israelites had gathered for worship. The sanctuary is to be destroyed together with the worshippers. Those who are lucky enough to escape the falling masonry would be killed by the sword in war. There was no escape for anyone.

Amos 9:2–4. God's omnipresence

It is impossible to escape from Yahweh, neither in she'ol (hell) nor heaven. Carmel with its thick forests and hidden caves was a good hiding ground but not from God. Nor was it possible to hide at the bottom of the sea since God's power was there also ruling mythological sea monsters. He will even be with them when they go into exile and will be responsible for their deaths. God chose Israel for responsibility and not for a privilege (9:7). Israel has abused this relationship and is no more a chosen nation than the Philistines or the Syrians. It is true that God brought the Israelites out of Egypt but he also brought the Philistines from Caphtos (Crete) and the Syrians (Arameans) from Kir. Amos is not rejecting the covenant relationship but Israel's misuse of it.

Amos 9:5–6

This is the third of the doxologies (4:13; 5:8–9) which come from a later hand than Amos; this one describes God's power in the universe.

Amos 9:8–18

The concluding section 8–18 has a messianic ring about

it and it could be a later addition by editors who wanted
Amos' book to end on a hopeful note. But we cannot rule
out the possibility that the optimism may be Amos' own.
'I will not utterly destroy the house of Jacob' (8) is
similar to the Isaian idea of the remnant and is a
qualification of Amos' earlier statements. Verse 9 is
ambiguous; is it a promise or a threat? Is what remains
in the sieve to be punished or saved? 'In that day I will
raise up the booth of David which is fallen' (9:11) seems
to presuppose the fall of Jerusalem (587 BC) and to
anticipate the rebuilding of the Davidic empire. This
verse seems to point to a post-exilic date for this passage.
The final description of the restoration and the accompanying marvellous material prosperity contains many
features of messianic literature.

5

Hosea's marriage
Hos 1:1–3:5

Introduction to Hosea: the interpretation of the marriage sections

As with Amos we have no knowledge of Hosea apart from what can be learnt from his book. We know that he was the son of Beeri (1:1) and that he lived in a village or town in the northern kingdom. We may assume that his prophetic ministry began in the reign of Jeroboam II, king of Israel (1:1) and continued into the troubled years which followed his reign. Under Jeroboam II (783–743) the northern kingdom of Israel saw her greatest days in terms of material prosperity and territorial expansion. Revolutionary intrigues and palace assassinations dominated the twenty years between the death of Jeroboam and the downfall of the kingdom. Jeroboam's son, Zechariah, was murdered by a certain Shallum after reigning for about six months. Shallum reigned for a month before Menahem, who managed to keep the throne from 745–738, killed him. This was the king who had to accept Assyrian overlordship from Tiglath-pileser III (745–727), a strong king who came to power at the same time as Jeroboam II died, and to pay heavy taxes (2 Kgs 15:19–26). His son Pekahiah had ruled Israel for a couple of years when he was murdered by Pekah, the leader of the anti-Assyrian movement.

29

Pekah took the Israelite throne. Pekah's other mistake was to form an alliance with Damascus against Judah, the southern kingdom. His aim was to rid Judah of the Davidic dynasty in favour of a king of the anti-Assyrian party. Ahaz, king of Judah, in spite of warnings from the prophet Isaiah, appealed to Assyria. Tiglath-pileser jumped at the opportunity to intervene and came to help (2 Kgs 16:5–9). He replaced Pekah with Hoshea who was pro-Assyrian and took Galilee and Transjordan from Israel. After Tiglath's death Hoshea joined Assyria's enemies. He was captured; Israel eventually fell in 722–721 and the people were dragged off into exile.

Hosea's book falls into two parts. Chapters 1–3 might be called biographical and belong to the early part of his ministry. The second part (4–14) is a collection of his prophetic oracles. It seems likely that the book was either written by Hosea himself or by some disciples of his shortly after his death. The Hebrew text is damaged in parts, which accounts for some of the obscurities and difficulties in translation.

The first three chapters set the tone for the rest of the book. They deal with Israel's unfaithfulness to Yahweh throughout their history and the analogy is drawn with the idea of an unfaithful wife. These chapters tell of a marriage between Hosea, the prophet, and Gomer, the prostitute; some scholars take this literally while others maintain that it was a vision or an allegory or parable. The main objection to literal interpretation of the narrative is the idea of God compelling anyone, especially a prophet, to do such a repulsive thing. But this objection could also be applied to the allegorical interpretation. There are no indications in the text that Hosea intended us to understand his marriage as anything but real. Among those scholars who take the narrative at face value some suggest that Hosea did not realise that Gomer was a prostitute until after his marriage and that when he discovered the fact he interpreted it as part of God's plan for him. Whether Hosea actually married a prostitute or not is not so important as the way he uses it to teach the Israelites that their unfaithfulness to Yahweh was no less shameful than the behaviour of an adulterous wife to a constant and loving husband.

Hos 1:1

The superscription or title is probably the work of an editor of a later time than Hosea. The series of kings of Judah (Uzziah to Hezekiah) covers the years 781–687 BC while Jeroboam II reigned from 783–743.

Hos 1:2–9. Hosea's marriage with Gomer

This account, in 1:2–9, is written in the third person while chapter 3, which is regarded by some scholars as a second account of the same experience and not as some kind of reconciliation, is written in the first person.

'Go take yourself a wife of harlotry. . . .' The meaning of 'a wife of harlotry' has been questioned. Gomer is called a harlot or prostitute, not an adulteress. It is possible that she was one of the sacred prostitutes at a Baal shrine. Worship of Baal was the practice of the Canaanites; many Israelites tried to worship both Baal, whose rituals involved orgies, and Yahweh. A second interpretation which has been suggested is that idolatry itself was called harlotry; Gomer could have been called a harlot simply because she, like many Israelites, had forsaken Yahweh and joined the worshippers of Baal. Some commentators maintain that the mention of the harlot's name, 'Gomer the daughter of Diblaim' (1:3) indicates that the prophet's story was not an allegory.

After the marriage a son was born to Gomer and Hosea (1:3). God told Hosea to call him Jezreel. The fact that Yahweh gave the child the name indicates that the child is a sign of God's will. 'Jezreel' means 'God scatters'. The dynasty of Jehu (the kings of Israel including Jeroboam II and his son) are to be punished for the 'blood of Jezreel', 1:4. Jezreel was a plain between Galilee, Samaria and the Jordan and was the scene of the massacre of the sons of Ahab, the Omrid dynasty: it is described in 2 Kgs 9–10. It is not just the dynasty of Jehu that is to be punished but the whole kingdom will lose its independence.

The second child of Hosea and Gomer was a daughter to whom God gave the name Lo-ruhama which means 'not pitied'. She symbolised God's intention not to forgive Israel; he will have no pity on them. 1:7, which maintains that God will pity and save Judah, is usually rejected as a later insertion by an editor who sympathised with Judah.

The third child (1:9) another son, God called Lo-ammi ('Not my people'). The Israelites had ceased to be his people and he was no longer their God.

Hos 1:10–2:1. A promise of restoration

This too is probably a later insertion. It seems to be a deliberate reversal of the preceding threats. The people are to increase and to be called 'sons of the living God' which is a reversal of 'not my people'. The two kingdoms, Judah and Israel, are to be reunited under one ruler whom they will elect and who will lead them to victory at Jezreel.

In Hosea's time sexual immorality went hand in hand with idolatry. Are there any reasons to support the view that current sexual permissiveness is related to abandonment of religion?

Hos 2 : 2–13. Israel's unfaithfulness to Yahweh

Israel has abandoned Yahweh for the Baalim. Her children, the unfaithful men of Israel are not Yahweh's children. God begs the children to plead with their mother, that is the men of Israel to plead with the nation, to put an end to this harlotry or idolatry. The stripping mentioned in 2:3 of clothes and jewels appears to have been a punishment of adultery (see Ezek 16:39). The children (2:4) are children of harlotry, not adultery because their mother, Israel, is a harlot. Her lovers (2:5) are the Baalim, whom she sees as her providers. Therefore 2:6 marks the change from accusation to judgement. She will find thorns instead of fruit trees and will not be able to find her way to the Baalim. The purpose of this is to make her return to her first love, Yahweh. Israel does not know that it was Yahweh who gave her prosperity, including the wine, oil, grain, silver and gold which she used in her false worship (2:8). As punishment God would take away her prosperity and put an end to her worship of the Baalim.

What is the real objection to idolatry? Is it just a more primitive type of religion? What would constitute idolatry today: for the church; for the individual; for society?

Hos 2:14–23. Israel's restoration

Yahweh will draw his bride back into the wilderness and re-teach her all the things she learned on their honeymoon, in the early days of the covenant relationship which followed the departure from Egypt. Here, the wilderness (2:14) probably means 'exile'. The Valley of Achor spelt trouble for the Israelites when they first entered the land of Canaan (Jos 7:26) but when they enter it the second time it will be a sign of new hope. The Hebrew words *ishi* and *baal* both meant 'my husband' but 'baal' is to be abandoned because of its association with the Baalim. Israel must forget Baal. On that day (2:16–18) when Yahweh saves his people he will make a covenant between Israel and creation. He will abolish war. In 2:19 the covenant continues in terms of marriage, a covenant made in righteousness, justice, in steadfast love and mercy. God will put an end to the drought and famine (2:21–22). The concluding verse is a reversal of 1:6 and 1:9; God will have pity on his people.

Hos 3:1–5. Hosea and his wife

This could be a second account, Hosea's own, of the events in 1:2–9, but it could also be a continuation of the story begun in 1:2. Yahweh commanded Hosea to love a woman who is an adulteress. Her adultery might only be in the general sense of unchastity but an adulteress in the strict sense is a more meaningful symbol for the unfaithful behaviour of Israel, since Israel forsook Yahweh after he had chosen her. Hosea buys Gomer the harlot but it is uncertain whether he pays the price of a slave or the usual bride price. It has been suggested, by those who maintain that chapter 3 is a continuation of the story and not a repetition of 1:2–9, that Hosea on finding that Gomer had been unfaithful to him had put her away, even sold her into slavery as a punishment; now he is commanded by God to buy her back. The wife has to dwell in seclusion for many days, possibly for punishment or retraining, but more probably because her association with pagan rites had made her too unclean to mix with worshippers of Yahweh. She must put an end to prostitution and adultery. One rendering of 'so will I also be to you' (3:3) is that Hosea the husband will have no intercourse with her during the days of seclusion. The marriage story ends here and the parallel with Israel is taken up. Israel's seclusion (3:4) will be the coming exile; she will lose her rulers and her religious rites, both Yahwistic and pagan. But her exile will be temporary; she will return and the Israelites will seek Yahweh. The reference to 'David, their king' (3:8) is probably not authentic, but illustrates Hosea's idea of restoration in terms of reunion under one leader.

Does the metaphor of Israel's unchastity help us to understand better the catholic tradition of the perpetual virginity of Mary?

6

Oracles against Israel
Hos 4:1–9:9

This section is a collection of the prophet's oracles which appear to be grouped according to subject rather than chronologically. It is in this section of the book of Hosea that the text is corrupt, and for this reason some scholars have denied the authenticity of references to Judah, to the restoration of Israel and the reunification of both kingdoms under the Davidic monarchy.

The first of this collection of oracles is a group which had sin and the need for repentance as its theme.

Hos 4:1–19. The sin of the people
Yahweh has a quarrel with the inhabitants of Israel; they are unfaithful, unpitying and ignorant of God (4:1). They no longer know Yahweh and the entire nation is corrupted by unlimited lying, stealing, killing and adultery; every law is broken. Because of this the whole land, including both men and animals, would endure drought and famine (4:3). The Hebrew of verse 4 is uncertain but the point seems to be that the priests were as guilty as the people. Nor were the prophets, not Hosea, but the professional sort, without sin (4:5); corrupt prophets were not uncommon. The reference to 'your mother' (4:5) probably means the land (cf 2:2). It is

37

lack of knowledge of Yahweh which leads man to sin
(4:6). Verses 7–8 refer to the fact that the priests
encouraged the Israelites to sin with their wrong ideas of
Yahweh because they gained materially by it. Both
priests and people will be punished.

It is as if the people were stupid with drink (4:11)
when they seek advice from wooden idols and oracles
from 'their staff'—a kind of tree oracle popular in
Israel for a long time. High places, like hill tops, and the
green groves of trees often housed sanctuaries for
Baalim (4:13). The worship of the Baalim involved
sacred prostitution; this was part of the fertility cult. The
significance of 'I will not punish . . .' (4:14) is that
among the Hebrews unchastity in women was severely
punished, but not in men. The people are not instructed
in knowledge of Yahweh and have forsaken him for the
Baalim.

The text of the next oracle (4:15–19) is corrupt and
therefore interpretation is difficult. The reference to
Judah is sometimes rejected as a late insertion though it
is found in some ancient versions of the Hebrew text.
Gilgal and Bethaven (perhaps an ironical name, meaning
'house of delusion', for Bethel) were famous sanctuaries
of the northern kingdom, well known for their association
with pagan practices. 'As the Lord lives' (4:15–16) is
thought to be a Baalistic cult formula to bring the
return of the god. Israel was so associated with idols that
she was to be left to them (4:17). A wind (spirit) has
moved them to idolatry; this will bring material as well
as spiritual ruin.

*If sin arises through ignorance of God how can the sinner be
held responsible?*

Hos 5:1–14. Charges against priests and rulers of Israel

The people have been trapped in sin by their priests and rulers; they as well as the people have been unfaithful to Yahweh. The priests and rulers will not escape judgement (5:1). Mizpah was in Gilead and Tabor in the north; they may have been centres of idolatry but we cannot tell from the context. Shittim was the place where the Israelites were literally seduced into false worship by the daughters of Moab (Num 25). Ephraim was the biggest tribe of the northern kingdom and it often represents the whole nation. Israel is defiled, that is, ritually unfit to draw near to Yahweh, but it is their sin more than their uncleanness which keeps the Israelites from him. The impulse which drives them to idolatry has made them forget God. God's patience has come to an end; he will withdraw from the people and when they seek him they will not be able to find him (5:5–7).

Gibeah and Ramah (5:8) were villages of the tribe of Benjamin near Jerusalem on the border between Israel and Judah. They originally belonged to the south but they may well have been annexed to the north in the eighth century. These villages would be the first to feel an attack from Judah. The day of punishment was the day of judgement which Israel deserved. Again the reference to the princes of Judah may not be authentic. It seems that Judah is the instrument of Israel's punishment and is therefore also to be punished. Judah had violated the deuteronomic law of the covenant by removing the boundary stones (Deut 27:17). Israel suffers because she was determined to go after idols. The implication of 5:12 is that Yahweh is present to destroy Israel and Judah, not to save them.

The Hebrew's misfortunes are described as an illness and for a cure they sought the advice of the Assyrian king. This in itself was a sin because it represented a lack of total trust in Yahweh. Besides this, ancient political alliances frequently involved the worship of the over-lord's gods. No political alliance could rescue Israel from her punishment. Yahweh, like a ravaging lion, would carry them off.

Was it realistic to expect Israel to avoid the security of foreign alliances? What about collective security today?

Hos 5:15–6:3. The Israelites seek forgiveness

Israel realises that her punishment is from God and seeks him out for forgiveness (6:1). The reference to 'two days' and on 'the third day' (6:2) indicate a short but indefinite period of time. 'Revive us' and 'raise us up' are references to the healing of the wounds which brought them near to death and not to resurrection from the dead. although if the repentance was genuine this event was like a raising to new life. The church fathers saw this passage as a foretelling of Christ's resurrection and the resurrection of all who believed in him. The phrase 'on the third day' might in fact be an allusion to the dying and rising cult of the fertility gods. It has also been suggested that the passage 5:15–6:3 is a quotation from a temple psalm which Hosea uses for the text of the con-demnation which follows.

Do christians give the impression of having 'come alive' through their sharing in Christ's risen life?

Hos 6:4–7:2. Repentance must be sincere

The rhetorical question 'What shall I do with you, O

Ephraim? What shall I do with you, O Judah?' illustrates Hosea's idea of the conflict between Yahweh's
desire to save and his desire for justice. Yahweh knows how
sincere is the repentance of the preceding passage and
how long it will last. Israel has not understood Yahweh
despite the hard lessons he had taught them through the
prophets. God's judgement is symbolised by the never
failing light of the sun in contrast to Israel's penitence
which is described as 'dew', something which comes and
goes. God desires love and knowledge rather than
sacrifice.

We do not know what covenant the Israelites broke
at Adam but possibly it refers to their betrayal of the
covenant when they entered Canaan and began to
indulge in the pagan rites. The Hebrew word 'adam' can
mean 'land' or 'country'; it has also been put forward
that this is a reference to Adan, a town in Transjordan.
When Hosea says that Gilead was 'tracked with blood'
he meant that it was a city full to the brim with crimes of
violence. Shechem was an ancient sanctuary and popular
with pilgrims, but the road to it was patrolled by
villainous highwaymen. Verse 11, with its reference to
Judah, could be a late gloss. 'Harvest' in this context
means judgement. The next verse summarises the thought
of the section; God wants to save his people but their
wickedness prevents him.

*If God really wants to save his people and he knows in
advance what they will do, then is not the ultimate responsibility
for their wickedness his?*

Hos 7:3–12. The monarchy is corrupt

The monarchy is condemned on two points; the court

intrigues and assassinations (7:3–7) and the seeking of
foreign alliances (8–12). Hosea was not condemning the
monarchy itself but the Israelite abuse of it. The princes
mentioned in 7:3 were probably the court officials who
were responsible for the organisation of the affairs of
state. The 'day of the king' was probably the day when
he was crowned: the courts were not only places of
political intrigue but also of excessive sensual pleasure.
It was among the court princes that palace coups were
plotted; the last kings of Israel had short, tragic reigns
ending in violence (7:7).

Turning to the subject of foreign alliances, Israel is
described as a 'half baked cake'. People of the ancient
east baked their bread and cakes on heated stones and if
they did not turn the food over it was baked on one side
only. These foreign alliances are useless, they make
Israel weaker not stronger (7:9). The 'grey hairs', a sign
of old age, illustrate this. The whole policy of seeking
pacts with Assyria and Egypt is condemned (7:11) and
the Israelites will be punished for seeking them and not
Yahweh (7:12).

Hos 7:13–16. A lament over Israel

Hosea bewails the fall of Israel. The lament as a literary
convention is quite common in prophetic writings, but
not in Hosea, which makes it more emphatic here. The
cause of their downfall is not their political assassinations
nor foreign alliances but their involvement in the worship of the Baalim. 'Redeem' (7:13) is a reference to
buying back or ransoming a slave's freedom. The
Israelite 'lies' were the insincere expressions of repentance; they were not genuine cries 'from the heart'.
'Waiting upon their beds' and 'gashing themselves' are

probably references to cultic practices of Baalism. In the past God led Israel in war to victory but now she has turned from him and seeks help elsewhere. The Israelites who worship Baal are described as a 'treacherous bow' (7:16) that is, a slack bow which will not shoot when needed. Israel was the instrument of God's plan but now she is condemned because she is unfaithful.

Hos 8:1–14. The invasion draws nearer

This chapter begins with a foretelling of war, the coming doom of Israel. The trumpet call was one to war (8:1). The vulture over the house of Israel is Assyria. This war is Israel's punishment for abandoning Yahweh.

The next section (8:4–7) links the making of kings with idolatry. These kings were made without Yahweh's approval. The golden bulls which Jeroboam I established at Israelite shrines are condemned (8:5–6); they are not God but the work of men's hands. The golden bulls themselves were not originally objects of worship but were looked upon as thrones of Yahweh's invisible presence. Some commentators think that here Hosea is not just condemning the worship of the bulls but the establishment of the northern kingdom.

Israel's idolatry is useless; it is like the whirlwind which wrecks the ripe grain (8:7–8). Hosea yet again condemns the foreign alliances, describing Israel as 'a wild ass' (8:9–10). Israel has built many altars and used them for idolatry (8:11). They appear to have ignored the written Hebrew laws about the building of altars (8:8–12). These sacrifices which the Israelites love to make do not please Yahweh. Hosea, like Amos, condemns the building of luxurious houses at the expense of the poor.

*Would the building of luxurious houses not have provided
employment for the poor? Are Amos and Hosea unfair over this?
Do luxury items still contribute to the impoverishment of others?*

Hos 9:1–9. Further oracles

This section is another collection of oracles concerning
Israel's crime and her doom. The first oracle denies
Israel the joy of the religious festivals, including the grain
and wine harvests. 'The peoples', that is the surrounding
nations, are not to be part of this gloomy picture since it
is only Israel and not they who have been unfaithful to
Yahweh. In a sense the nations could not be unfaithful to
Yahweh because he had not chosen them as he had
elected Israel. The oracle goes on to relate that in fact
there will be nothing to rejoice over; there will be no
harvests (9:2) for Israel will be in exile in Assyria (9:3).
No-one was taken captive into Egypt but some sought it
as a place of safety. The Israelite return to Egypt
represented a reversal of the salvific event of the exodus.
The Israelites' food in Assyria would be unclean because
it had been produced in an unclean land and not in the
land of Yahweh. This ritually unclean food could not be
offered as sacrifice to Yahweh: this is why the sacrificial
worship ceased while the Israelites were in exile (9:4).
Verse 5 is a rhetorical question; there would be no
festival and no day of the Lord in exile. The land of
Israel itself will be desolate, weeds growing over the
silver.

The days of punishment have come (9:7); this is an
example of the 'prophetic perfect'—Israel's doom is so
certain that it is already spoken of as fact. 'The prophet
is a fool' is most probably a gibe from the people. Hosea
had invited rejection by criticising the cult. In 1 Sam

10:9–13 the Israelites thought that the prophets were madmen. Israel had rejected prophets and their messages on many occasions. The prophet was really Israel's watchman; it was he who watched for danger and gave warnings but he met opposition (9:8). The oracle concludes with a typical condemnation.

Should christians appear as 'fools' in modern society or should they be practical and be prepared to accept moral compromise?

7

Israel, past and present
Hos 9:10–14:9

Hos 9:10–17. God's relations with Israel

When Yahweh chose Israel, at the beginning of their
history, he was delighted with them; it was the un-
expected discovery of grapes in the wilderness or like the
first ripe fruit of the fig tree (9:10). The Israelites soon
spoilt this by abandoning Yahweh for the worship of the
Canaanite Baalim (cf Num 25). Therefore there will be
no future for Israel; she would decline. No children
would be born to her women and grown-up children
would be killed in battle (9:11–13). Worst of all, God
will abandon them (9:12). Gilgal (9:15), which was full
of Israel's evil, was probably the shrine near Jericho.
The references to Baalpeor and Gilgal are thought to
recall the conquest of the land of Canaan. Israel will
be punished for her unfaithfulness by depopulation and
exile. Verse 17, like verse 14, is Hosea's comment on
God's words (9:10–13 and 15–16).

*Is reflection on the past, in the style of this and the following
sections, of any value? Shouldn't we forget the past?*

Hos 10:1–9. Prosperity is dangerous

Israel is described in this oracle as a vine, a very fruitful

47

one. But the more Israel's prosperity increased the more
she sinned. More altars and cultic objects were built. The
Israelite worship is false; God will destroy it. The complaint that they have no king (10:3) could be a reference
to the exile where there was no king in fact, or to the
ineffectiveness of the king's rule. The covenants mentioned in 10:4 are not religious but political alliances or
treatises. The golden calf, worshipped in Samaria since
Jeroboam 1 established it, is to be carried off into exile.
The Israelites will mourn for it even though it has failed
them (10:5). The king, cult and people of Israel will
disappear from the land. The land will be desolated, no
one will want to survive in it but rather cry to it for
burial (10:8).

*Can the decline in religious observance today be blamed on
increased prosperity? If so, why?*

Hos 10:9–15. Israel's sin

Israel's sin goes back to very early times. There are three
suggested interpretations of 'from the days of Gibeah'
which is the episode from which Israel's sin is supposed
to date. First of all there is the reference to Gibeah in
Jgs 19–20 where the eleven tribes (Israel) take vengeance on
one tribe (the Benjamites) for some crime; this episode
does not fit since it is not Israel who sins. The second
suggestion is the beginning of the monarchy under Saul
which took place at Gibeah. It is possible that Hosea
regarded the monarchy as a sin but more likely that
Hosea was opposed to division into two kingdoms
rather than to the establishment of one. A third solution
is the idolatry of Micah (Jgs 17:1–6) which was the
traditional beginning of idolatry among the Israelites.

The punishment for this sin is defeat in war. God will punish the unrighteous. The nations will gather against them. Hosea usually names the enemy, either Assyria or Egypt, but no indication is given here of the enemies' identity. There is some question concerning the meaning of their double iniquity (10:13). It could possibly mean the idolatry of Micah and of Jeroboam; or the golden calves at Bethel and Dan; or the abandonment of Yahweh and the acceptance of idols.

In the next verse (10:11) Israel is compared to a young heifer who is accustomed to the easy job of walking round and round the threshing floor. As no muzzle was allowed to be worn for this task (Deut 25:4) the animal could eat freely. It was nice work. Her neck had not been marked by the heavy yoke that oxen wore for ploughing and reaping. But the time had come for Israel to do these heavier, harder tasks. The prophet then demands that Israel should do three things. The Israelites must 'sow righteousness'; they must let justice govern their dealings with other men. Secondly, they must 'reap the fruit of steadfast love'; their lives must be filled with love, and their actions marked by love. Finally, the Israelites must 'break up their fallow ground'. Before the seed can be sown, neglected ground, full of weeds and thorns, has to be prepared; the Israelites must abandon the old ways of sin before they can start a new life with Yahweh whom Hosea thinks will save the Israelites if they do these things. The farming metaphor is continued to describe Israel's sin (10:13). Because they trusted in warfare instead of Yahweh their punishment will be destruction by war (10:14). 'As Shalman destroyed Betharbel on the day of battle' has been the subject of much conjecturing. The most probable suggestion for the identification of Shalman is Shalmanezer IV who became king of Assyria

in 727 BC and beseiged Samaria in 724–722 BC. Betharbel
has been identified with the Assyrian Arbel on the Tigris
but this site was probably too far away to make much
impression on the Israelites. A more likely suggestion is
Arbela on the west of the sea of Tiberias. The actual
incident referred to is unknown. An alternative reading
to 'in the storm' (10:15) is 'at dawn', which gives an
impression of the suddenness of the attack on the
Israelite king.

*Can we really see idolatry as the fundamental sin today? Is
Hosea's idea of genuine repentance adequate for christians?*

Hos 11:1–11. God's justice and his love for Israel

The beginning of the chapter sees a return to Hosea's
idea of the love/marriage relationship between Yahweh
and Israel. Israel was young when God first chose her.
He trained the Israelites lovingly like a father, but they
soon turned from him to idolatry (11:1–4). The Israelites'
punishment for refusing to return to Yahweh is to be
exiled; the mention of Egypt and Assyria seems to imply
a double exile. Many will fall in battle (11:6) and be
yoked like oxen (11:7). As the inevitable doom approaches
the prophet again expresses God's love. There is a
conflict in Hosea's mind between God's hungering love
for his people and his justice. How can he give up
Israel (11:8)? 'Admah' and 'Zeboim' were cities of the
plain destroyed with Sodom and Gomorrah (Gen 14:2–8).
It has been suggested that verse 9 is an interpolation, or
that it should be read as a question, eg 'will I not?'
rather than 'I will not...'. 'For I am God and not
man...' seems to imply that God's purpose cannot be
shaken; that his justice must be vindicated. The con-

cluding verses of this section (11:10–11) look forward
hopefully to a return to Yahweh and a return from exile.

*Do we need the concept of God's justice as well as his love?
Are they really two different qualities?*

Hos 11:12–12:14. Israel's falseness

Yahweh cannot escape from Israel's lies and deceitful-
ness (11:12). The Israelites also rely on things that
deceive, like treaties with Assyria and Egypt. The
description of Israel herding the wind instead of a flock,
and hunting the sirocco, the deadly south-east wind,
alludes to the emptiness and meaninglessness of all her
endeavours. The reference to Judah's faithfulness (11:12)
and to her punishment (12:2) may be later insertions.
Jacob was Israel's ancestor and according to tradition he
supplanted his twin brother while still in their mother's
womb (Gen 25). This characteristic in this deceitful and
untrustworthy nation now has to be punished. The
references in 12:3–5 are to events in the cycles of stories
concerning Jacob in Genesis (Gen 25:24; 32:24; 35:9).
The whole passage (12:5–6) seems to teach that God
can be approached as of old.

Israel is like a cheating merchant but their riches cannot blot out their guilt (12:7–8). 'I will again make you
dwell in tents'; this could be a promise or a threat. If we
take it as a promise it means leaving the degrading
present way of life and returning to the simple life of the
early days of Israel's history. This interpretation implies
that civilisation is a curse, an evil. On the other hand if
we look upon Yahweh's words as a threat it means that
the Israelites will again be compelled to leave their
homes for nomadic lives in the wilderness. The next line,

'as in the days of the appointed feast', could be a reference to the feast of tabernacles which was a thanksgiving for the harvest and in later times was looked upon as a reminder of the early days of Jewish history.

God sent plenty of warnings to his people through his prophets (12:10). The text of the next verse is corrupt but it concerns the idolatry at Gilead and Gilgal which will be destroyed. Verse 12 is misplaced; it is part of the Jacob story and obviously belongs with 12:3–6. The prophet who brought Israel out of Egypt was Moses (12:13). Israel has provoked God; she will be punished.

Hos 13. Israel is doomed

In the past Israel was great and respected by the surrounding nations but because of their ever-increasing idolatry they will disappear from the face of the earth like mist or dew in the early morning, or like chaff from the threshing floor or smoke from a window (13:1–3). It was Yahweh who had brought the Israelites from Egypt; he is their only God and saviour. It was this God who looked after them during their wanderings in the desert, leading them to food and water. But despite all this Israel was ungrateful. Hosea portrays Yahweh suddenly turning on them like some wild animal and tearing them to pieces (13:4–8).

There is no-one to rescue Israel from her punishment. The Israelite kings are powerless to help. Verse 11 suggests that the series of short reigns ending in violence was regarded, at least by Hosea, as a sign of Yahweh's disapproval. Israel's sin is stored up, like money in bags, ready to be produced as evidence of their guilt on the day of judgement. A common old testament metaphor for distress was the inévitable pain and discomfort of a woman in labour. In this case the fact that the woman is depicted as unable to give birth to her child emphasises that there is no escape from Israel's punishment. Israel fails to be born again to new life with Yahweh.

Hosea cannot conceive of Yahweh rescuing the sinful Israelites from death or she'ol (the Hebrew underworld); their sin is too great. 'O death where are your plagues? O She'ol, where is your destruction?' is the passage quoted in 1 Cor 15:55 in triumph over death, but here it is more probably an appeal to death to bring forth its miseries (13:14). It is as if compassion was hidden from Yahweh's eyes; Israel will perish as the land perishes when scourged by the sirocco (13:15). The east wind here represents Assyria. The northern kingdom's punishment for sin is defeat and death, even of the unborn, in war.

If God is unable to reason man from sin would it not be more loving for him to make some miraculous intervention rather than to leave him to the terrible consequences of sin?

Hos 14. A promise of forgiveness

Many scholars reject this chapter as a late addition. It is thought to be prophetic work from a later time, probably after the exile. But it has also been suggested that Hosea addressed this last chapter to the Israel of the future; to the remnant who would survive the Assyrian exile. Some commentators who support this view maintain that the style and language of the chapter, with the exception of the last verse, is that of Hosea himself.

The writer of this chapter entreats his readers to drink well of the lesson of the fate of the Israelites. The tense of 'you have stumbled' presupposes the fall of the northern kingdom. Those who wish to return to Yahweh must do so with genuine penitence (14:2) and they must trust in God alone, not in Assyria, nor in the Egyptian cavalry, nor in the idols they made in the past. The sentence 'In thee the orphan finds mercy' (14:3) seems to be misplaced here; it reads better at the end of the second verse.

Assured of Israel's repentance, Yahweh, through the prophet, promises forgiveness (14:4). The restoration (14:4–8) is described in the beautiful imagery, taken from nature, which is used frequently throughout biblical writings. The last verse, an appeal to the wise to understand, is similar to many exhortations found in the wisdom literature, for example, Prov 11:5, 15:19, and Ecclus (Sir) 39:24, and almost certainly a later addition.

Does the church have lessons to learn from defeats and reverses? How far was the protestant reformation a judgement upon the spiritual failure of catholicism? Can the atheism of communist regimes be viewed as a judgement on the church's lack of concern with social justice?

Isaiah 1–39

Joseph Rhymer

Introduction:
Reading Isaiah 1–39

The ministry of Isaiah of Jerusalem spanned more than fifty years from about 740 BC, 'the year that King Uzziah died' (Is 6:1), to the early years of King Manasseh, who became king of Judah in 687 BC. During this half century the Hebrew people experienced political, social and religious changes which were as great and as disturbing as the changes which have occured in Europe during the first half of the twentieth century AD, and which were as far-reaching in their effects. Is 1–39 will make very little sense unless it is read with this background in mind.

The book of Isaiah bears the marks of the turbulent period in which it was compiled. It contains material written or spoken over a period of at least two hundred years, and repeatedly edited before it reached the form in which we now have it. Again, to appreciate the significance of this material it is important to see it within the context of other old testament writings of the same period. In the following arrangement the various elements of Is 1–39 are listed along with contemporary old testament material. Although it may seem complex at first sight, reading the book within this context will richly repay the trouble involved. The Isaiah references are in italics.

1 Kgs 12–2 Kgs 14:29 (The animosity between the two Hebrew kingdoms from the death of Solomon to the beginning of Uzziah's reign)

Amos

Hosea

2 Kgs 15:1–38 (The opening of Isaiah's ministry)

Is 1–6

2 Kgs 16:1–17:41 (The destruction of the northern Hebrew kingdom)

Is 7–12

Is 17:1–11

Is 28:1–29

Is 29:15–24

Micah

2 Kgs 18:1–20:21 (The reign of Hezekiah)

Is 20:1–6

Is 21:11–23:18

Is 29:1–14

Is 30:1–18

Is 30:27–32:14

(*Is 36:1–38:8* and *39:1–8*, which are almost identical with 2 Kgs 18:1–20:21)

Is 14:24–16:14

Is 17:12–19:15

2 Kgs 21:1–22:2 (The reign of Manasseh to the opening of Josiah's reign)

Deuteronomy

Zephaniah

Nahum

Jeremiah

Habakkuk

Ezekiel

Is 13:1–14:23

Is 19:16–25

Is 21 : 1–10
Is 30 : 19–26
Is 32 : 15–35 : 10

The remaining material consists of Is 24–27, which is an apocalyptic section, and Is 38:9–20, a section similar to some of the psalms. It is impossible to put a date to this material with any confidence, but both sections probably belong to the period after the return from the exile in Babylon, nearly two centuries after the ministry of Isaiah of Jerusalem.

It is obvious that there is a considerable amount of material here which does not even belong to the period of Isaiah. The simple explanation for this is to be found in the economical habits of Hebrew scribes, who used the spare space on the papyrus scrolls to preserve anonymous prophetic material. The final chapters of the book, Is 40–66, are the work of an anonymous prophet (or possibly two) at the end of the exile, usually referred to as Second Isaiah, or Isaiah of Babylon.

1. Since scripture is 'the word of God', why is it necessary to know anything about the situation in which it was originally written?

2. The church's teaching has frequently been expressed in the form of council decrees and encyclicals. To what extent can these be applied universally, or in a period other than the one in which they were formulated?

By 740 BC, when Isaiah started his ministry, the Hebrew people had been divided into two kingdoms for nearly two hundred years, and there was no sign that the division would be healed. The frontier crossed Palestine just to the north of Jerusalem, leaving the city as capital of the weaker, smaller and poorer southern kingdom of

Judah. The majority of the Hebrew people lived in the northern kingdom of Israel, with its capital at Samaria, and with two main centres of worship at Dan and Bethel to serve the religious needs of the north in place of Jerusalem. The division began at the death of Solomon, and created a situation similar to the two parts of Ireland in our times. The people looked back to David's reign as an ideal period, when the people were united, independant, and the dominant nation in the whole area of Palestine and Syria. The covenant with David (2 Sam 7) symbolised popular nostalgia for the period when undisputed and united possession of Palestine was the proof that the Hebrews were the specially chosen people of God. It also produced a deep complacency in the majority of the people, a complacency which survived even the most terrible experiences of national collapse.

Two dynamic prophets, Amos and Hosea, had preached in the northern Hebrew kingdom in the decade before Isaiah began his ministry in the southern kingdom, and although the two kingdoms were normally in a state of enmity the teaching of these prophets would have reached the southern kingdom as well. Moreover, the picture which emerges from the books of Amos and Hosea was broadly true of the southern kingdom as well as the northern one.

Amos had denounced the social situation in the northern kingdom with uncompromising clarity. The comparatively unstratified character of the old Hebrew pastoral way of life had changed radically. The economic prosperity of the northern kingdom produced wide differences between the rich and the poor; this was reflected in the law courts, where the infinite value of each human being and their equality before God had been forgotten, so that the poor could not obtain justice;

it was reflected in the emergence of a slave class who had no hope of regaining their economic freedom; and it was reflected in the religious attitudes of external observance and complacency, where the sacrificial cult was maintained to support the social system. Amos centred his teaching on the escape from Egypt, where the Hebrews had first realised that their God put his own value on each human being, and expected them to recognise this in each other.

Hosea had taken the understanding a stage further in the same northern kingdom, but with the emphasis on the relationship between the people's religious beliefs and the agricultural economy. The native religion of Palestine was a fertility cult with a host of minor gods and goddesses whose sexual intercourse controlled the fertility of people, animals and crops. Sacral prostitution played a large part in worship, and it is clear that a large proportion of the Hebrews accepted this form of worship along with the agricultural techniques which they learned from the native Palestinians.

Hosea denounced all this on the grounds that it failed to recognise that the Hebrew God was responsible for all aspects of life; creation is a continuous, dynamic process, and the only source of it is Yahweh. Hosea is notable for the vivid way in which his own personal experience led him to a deeper insight into God's relationship with his world. His wife deserted him and became a prostitute, probably one of the sacral prostitutes of the fertility cult. In his realisation that he was still anxious for her to return to him and renew the marriage, Hosea recognised that God was prepared to maintain and renew the covenant with an utterly dependable and deeply tender love. Hosea writes of the escape from Egypt and the journey through the wilderness as the honeymoon period, and begs the people to return to the God of creation and redemption who continually waits for their return to him.

Isaiah stood on the shoulders of Amos and Hosea, and so was able to see a little further than they could. It is worth noticing that neither Amos nor Hosea had any general success in their preaching, so far as we can tell. Their impact was on such like-minded successors as Isaiah, who understood the significance of their teaching, incorporated it into his own teaching, and developed it. Amos's insistence on God's righteousness, and Hosea's understanding of God's love, are both taken for granted in Isaiah. From them Isaiah develops his own unique understanding of God's holiness, and its relevance to national and personal life. In his turn, Isaiah was to have no more success than his predecessors, except in the profound influence his teaching had on Hebrew reformers long after his death. What Isaiah had to say was luminously clear and unmistakably relevant to his own times, but he was ignored.

1. What forms might prophecy be expected to take today?

2. What relationships have existed and might be expected to exist between prophecy and traditional religious organisations?

Book list

For anyone studying Isaiah's insights seriously, a good atlas of the ancient world, and a good history, are essential. The following will be found useful:

John Bright *A History of Israel* (scm Press)
Martin Noth *The History of Israel* (A. & C. Black).
Grollenberg *Atlas of the Bible* (Nelson).

To these I would add a good general commentary, particularly:

The Jerome Biblical Commentary (Chapman).

Of simple commentaries on Isaiah alone, or Isaiah and the other prophets of his time, I would suggest:

J. Rhymer *The Prophets and the Law* (Sheed & Ward).
G. Ernest Wright *Isaiah* (scm Press).

1

God's holiness: the vision in the temple
Is 6:1–13

Both the date (740 BC) and the contents of the events in this chapter show that it should be at the beginning of the book, for it sets the pattern of the whole of Isaiah's ministry. An editor has moved it here to form an introduction to the dramatic confrontation between Isaiah and King Ahaz recounted in Is 7–8, and the messianic teaching of the whole section Is 7–12, 'The Book of Immanuel'.

Is 6:1–4

The temple in Jerusalem was far more than a magnificent meeting place for worship, adjacent to the royal palace at the northern end of the narrow city; it was also a visual symbol in which a great range of beliefs and traditions about God were concentrated and given coherence. Architecturally it consisted of a dark inner room, the 'holy of holies', containing the ark of the covenant, which was approached from a larger sanctuary containing an altar of incense and the table of 'shew-bread' which symbolised the nation. A porch led from this sanctuary to a court with the altar of burnt offerings. The whole effect on the worshipper emphasised the power and mystery of God, and this was reinforced by the restrictions on access.

Only the high priest could enter the holy of holies, and that only once a year; laity worshipped from the court outside the large sanctuary.

From its beginnings in the reigns of David and Solomon, the temple had been a focus for the central religious traditions which had created the nation itself, for it was primarily built to house the sacred ark of the covenant. This was the portable shrine containing the tablets of the law. The people had brought it to Palestine after the escape from Egypt, for it symbolised the active presence of God, who still protected his people and fought for them, as at the exodus itself. The people thought of it as the throne of God and the place where they were most confident of his protective presence and saving power. The ark as a throne was called the 'expiatory', for it was the centre of justice and forgiveness. This is the background for the important passage in Romans, where Christ is presented as the redeemer 'whom God put forward as an expiation by his blood . . . to show God's righteousness, because in his divine forbearance he had passed over former sins' (Rom 3:25). In Isaiah's vision the seraphim represent the angelic court who proclaimed God's majesty and symbolised the subordination of every power in the universe to the power of God.

In the vision the song of the seraphim, 'Holy, holy, holy is the Lord of hosts; the whole earth is full of his glory', combines three aspects of God's relationship with the world. The basic meaning of 'holiness' is transcendence and separation from all imperfection. 'Lord of hosts' refers to God as the creator and leader of victorious armies, particularly the armies of Israel, of course. But the Hebrew God is also the only God; his power rules the whole world; wherever it is felt and recognised it creates the awe which is the human response to God's glory and is the basis of all worship.

At first sight there seems to be a contradiction between the concept of holiness as separation and the involvement in human affairs implied by armies and battles. The thread which links them, and which runs deeply throughout Isaiah's writings, is the concept of justice. This connection is basic to the central experience of Hebrew religion, where the Sinai covenant combines the divine initiative expressed in invincibly righteous power, and the human response shown through the laws which express right human relationships. This is vividly emphasised in Exodus 19–24, where the account of the experience of God's presence at Sinai also contains the ten commandments and the earliest collection of old testament law. The people must express God's character in their relationships with each other if they wish to enjoy the benefits of God's covenant with them. This fundamental connection between God's holiness and human responsibility is expressed in the Lord's prayer, and throughout Christ's teaching in such parables as the good Samaritan (Lk 10:25–37; Mt 6:9–15).

The transcendence and separation expressed in the holiness of God are absolute sources for justice which lift it away from all human imperfection and compromise. Human laws, and the decisions of government at every level, are all framed to meet the needs of a particular time and place. The laws in the bible are no exception to this. But they must all be tested against the absolute values which God places on human beings and which he has demonstrated in the great historical acts by which men have been given the opportunity of deliverance from their helplessness. Redemption is the human experience of God's holiness in action, meeting the human need and establishing right human relationships when men recognise it and cooperate with it. The life and work of Jesus Christ is the perfect demonstration of God's redemptive holiness and of human cooperation, and the crucifixion and resurrection show that God will not compromise, nor withdraw from the human situation, until the power of his holiness overcomes all that opposes it. Isaiah's realisation of God's holiness is the source of his conviction that the nation can only remain under the protection of the covenant if it expresses that holiness in its everyday life.

1. The language of Isaiah's vision suggests that it is situated in one of the normal services of the temple. What relationship should there be between routine christian worship and christian action in the everyday world? Do the forms and contents of christian worship help people to see the relevance of christianity in ordinary life? How could they be of greater help?

2. What criteria are there for deciding whether laws and administrative decisions are just? Whose responsibility is it to apply the criteria: the government's? the electorate's? the church's?

Is 6:5–13

The immediate reaction of Isaiah to the realisation of the presence and holiness of God was intense awareness of his own inadequacy: '... I am lost; for I am a man of unclean lips, and I dwell in the midst of a people of unclean lips' (Is 6:5). It is a reaction which can be parallelled in the call of Jeremiah, where the prophet pleads that he is too young for the terrible responsibility given to him (Jer 1:6), and of Peter. Luke's account of the call of Peter places it in the context of a miraculous catch of fish which shows the unusual powers of Jesus and, like Isaiah, Peter's recognition of his sinfulness was followed immediately by his call to be an apostle. This realisation of inadequacy and of sinfulness is a main theme of 2 Corinthians, where Paul discusses the essential qualifications of an apostle and concludes that it is to be found in 'weakness': '"My grace is sufficient for you, for my power is made perfect in weakness." I will all the more gladly boast of my weaknesses, that the power of Christ may rest upon me' (2 Cor 12:9, but see the whole passage from 2 Cor 10). The prophet and the apostle must see his situation from God's point of view, not his own, and rely on God's methods and the power of God's love.

After a cleansing symbolised by the burning coal taken from the altar (and the use of fire as a symbol of God's holiness and power has deep roots, as is shown by the part it played in sacrifice, by the derivation of 'seraph' from the Hebrew word for fire, and by its use in the new testament to convey the experience of the power of the Holy Spirit) Isaiah is given his responsibility. It is to preach ineffectively to a people who are only hardened and turned further from God by the preaching (Is 7:9–10). This passage is best seen as Isaiah's later reflections as he looked back on his ministry. At the moment of greatest national need, the king would refuse to take his advice and would make decisions which brought disaster to the nation; but even at the ordinary level, the century of social and moral degradation which followed Isaiah's ministry shows that his preaching had little effect.

There is a direct quotation from this passage in the parable of the sower (Mk 4:1–12), in which the hardest part of the passage is given by Jesus as the explanation of his teaching methods: 'To you (the apostles) has been given the secret of the kingdom of God, but for those outside everything is in parables; so that they may indeed see but not perceive, and may indeed hear but not understand; lest they should turn again and be forgiven' (Mk 4: 11–12). The emphasis is on the human responsibility to respond freely to the divine initiative in order to understand it, for without this freedom to respond—or to turn away and never understand—the relationship with God would be a forced one. Love requires that the relationship should be evoked by a genuinely free response to the divine initiative, with no element of constraint in it.

Yet the effects of ignoring the divine initiative are disastrous, for the person cannot remain unchanged by the presence of God. This theme runs right through John's gospel, where people judge themselves by their acceptance or rejection of Christ as he moves amongst them: 'He came to his own home, and his own people received him not. But to all who received him, who believed in his name, he gave power to become children of God . . .' (Jn 1:11–12). This experience lay at the heart of Isaiah's ministry, for he was aware that when he spoke in the name of God he released a power which could not leave the hearer unchanged.

In the course of his ministry Isaiah saw the greater part of the Hebrew people, the northern kingdom of Israel, eliminated, and Judah made a puppet of Assyria with the Assyrian religion and way of life stamped deeply into the people's lives. But there would still be sufficient response to preserve the accumulated Hebrew experience of God, even if it were only a small minority forced into silence and secrecy. The faithful in the nation would be 'like a terebinth or an oak, whose stump remains standing when it is felled. The holy seed is its stump' (Is 7:13). This remnant, composed of those who responded to God's holiness, is an important theme in Isaiah's writings.

1. If a sense of inadequacy is essential for a successful apostolate, how will this be shown in modern circumstances?

2. In what ways is the christian message being ignored by the majority of people today?

3. If Isaiah looked for a 'faithful remnant' today, where would he find it?

2

The early preaching:
Is 1–5

Is 1:1–4:1

The opening chapters of Isaiah are a fierce indictment of
the social and religious condition of Jerusalem, and of the
southern kingdom of Judah ruled and influenced by it.
'Indictment', with its legal overtones, is the right word,
for Isaiah uses a law court as a setting for his message;
God asks the whole of creation to be a jury, and to hear
his case against his chosen people: 'Hear, O heavens, and
give ear, O earth . . . Their partiality witnesses against
them . . . The Lord has taken his place to contend, he
stands to judge his people' (Is 1:2; 3:9, 13). The case is
overwhelming, yet these chapters are also full of the
opportunity God provides for full forgiveness and
restoration to complete fellowship with him. The insights
of Amos, with his emphasis on strict justice, and of Hosea,
with his realisation of God's steadfast faithfulness and
tender love, are combined by Isaiah. This is an excellent
example of the continuity and the development running
through all the main prophets of the old testament. Each
is able to see a little further because he is standing on the
shoulders of his predecessors, and this is why it is important to read the prophets (and the other books of the
bible) in the order in which they were written.

The heart of the people's offence is ingratitude towards

God and failure to realise how dependent they are on the continually creative power of God. God's sons have rebelled against him, and their lives have disintegrated into social injustice, luxury and arrogance. Isaiah uses the language of punishment to express this sequence, and so remains consistently within the legal metaphor which he has chosen, but the corruption of the people is really a causal consequence of their rejection of God: 'They have forsaken the Lord, they have despised the Holy One of Israel, they are utterly estranged' (Is 1:4). (There is an unavoidable ambiguity in the use of 'Israel'; sometimes it refers to the northern kingdom, as distinct from Judah, and sometimes it refers to the whole Hebrew people who trace their descent from Jacob-Israel, but the context usually makes the meaning clear.) This same causal sequence of rebellion followed by the disintegration of human relationships is the main point of the second creation narrative in Gen 2:4b–4:16, which was compiled about a century before Isaiah. There the attempt to exercise power independently of God (the Hebrew phrase 'knowledge of good and evil' is an idiom for power over everything that exists) leads to estrangement from God, to enmity and murder within the human family, and enmity with the rest of the natural world.

The result of rebellion from God is isolation for the nation and its members, like a shed or a tent in the middle of a field: ' . . . the daughter of Zion is left like a booth in a vineyard, like a lodge in a cucumber field, like a besieged city' (Is 1:8). Against this background of self-sufficiency the nation's religion becomes a meaningless blasphemy. The cult, with its sacrifices and sequence of religious festivals, was maintained faithfully in the temple and in the local Hebrew sacrificial centres throughout the country, but it had ceased to have any relevance to secular life. The religious life of the people could only be meaningful if they would '. . . cease to do evil, learn to do good; seek justice, correct oppression; defend the fatherless, plead for the widow' (Is 1:16-17).

Implicit in this is the problem of how this can be possible, once the people have turned away from God. This question had already been raised in Gen 6:5, 'every imagination of the thoughts of his (man's) heart was only evil continually' (where 'heart' symbolises the centre of personality where action originates); Isaiah recognised that only God can restore again (Is 4:4), but it was not until a century later that Jeremiah realised the full hopelessness of the human condition by looking forward to a new covenant in which human nature would be transformed and renewed (Jer 31:31-34). Meanwhile, Isaiah can only see a time of social disaster from which those who recognise the causes of it will emerge as a purified remnant to form the nucleus of a new people of God.

Palestine was a corridor country through which all the cultures of the Middle East passed. Consequently the Hebrews had allowed their religion to develop into a syncretism of elements borrowed from a wide range of religions. The indigenous religion of Palestine was a fertility cult derived from the agricultural economy, which the Hebrews also adopted when they slowly changed from their semi-nomadic pastoral way of life. The effects of all this were to fragment the supernatural powers which the people worshipped as the controlling forces in their lives (Is 2:6-8). The gods were departmentalised so that it was easy to ignore the essential connection between religion and morality. The monotheism which had always been implicit in the Hebrew religion emphasised that there was only one supreme power in the universe. If this was denied, by a religion which accepted the worship of many gods, there could be no single unifying principle in the complexity of human activities and relationships.

The clearest indications of this, for Isaiah, were the social disorders which he saw throughout the nation (Is 3:2–5), the oppression of the poor by the nation's rulers (Is 3:14–15), and the arrogant luxury of the rich (Is 3:16–26). There could be no cure for these disorders except the recognition that God alone is the source of all authority and power, and any attempt to wield these independently of God is bound to become corrupt.

1. Isolation and loneliness are an urgent modern problem, particularly in large cities. To what extent is this a sign of the failure to apply christianity, or are there other causes?

2. Is there a modern equivalent to the ancient fragmentation of life through polytheism? Are the multiplicity of christian denominations and sects a form of polytheism, with similar consequences?

Is 2:2–4; 4:2–5:30

In two notable passages in this early section of teaching, Isaiah weaves powerful themes of hope; the God whom the people have deserted, or treated so casually, is the source of all human satisfaction and he is anxious to bring his creation to the fulfilment for which he has made it. Such passages as Is 2:2–4 and 4:2–6 can be given a general title such as 'the messianic hope', but it would be a mistake to think that such a hope in a future golden age was ever completely clear in the old testament. Rather, a whole range of powerful images recur throughout the prophetic writings in a variety of combinations. They express the deepest confidence in God's power; his plan and purpose for his creation, and particularly for his chosen people, cannot be thwarted for ever.

Although there are brief passages expressing confidence in the future in Amos and Hosea (and a real possibility that they were inserted by later editors), Isaiah is the first prophet to produce such passages as a major part of his teaching. In 2:2–4, the hope is a universal one, attracting a world-wide response. It is centred on Jerusalem and its temple on Mount Zion, 'the mountain of the house of the Lord', but the main point is that all will be attracted to it and find there 'the law', 'the word of the Lord', true justice and a universal peace which will end all wars: 'they shall beat their swords into ploughshares, and their spears into pruning hooks'. 'Law', in the Hebrew sense, is something much wider than a system of laws and regulations. The first five books of the old testament are called 'the law' in Hebrew bibles, but they contain much historical material written to demonstrate the whole pattern of life of a people living in the covenant relationship with God. The holiness, love and power of God is revealed in the lives of the people whom he has chosen, when they respond to him. It is the pattern of this response, and the satisfaction which is to be found in it, which constitutes 'law'; the messianic hope looks forward to a time when all peoples will find it irresistibly attractive.

The later passage, Is 4:2–6, concentrates on the Hebrew people, but it introduces further vital elements in their hope. The remnant which survives the coming disasters will find that they are sharing in God's holiness, for God will purify them. Isaiah uses two of the powerful symbols that occur in the accounts of the deliverance from Egypt and the covenant at Sinai: the pillar of

cloud and the pillar of fire will cover the Jerusalem
temple in a canopy of glory. They will signify the
protecting presence of God, and the unassailable security
of a covenant which has been made effective in the
people's lives.

But these early chapters end on a note of condemnation
as Isaiah returns to the realities of the situation as he sees
it in his own times. Chapter 5 opens with the famous
'song of the vineyard', a parable of frustration. Judah is
like a vineyard on which every care and skill has been
lavished. It was planted with the finest stock, and given
every possible attention; but at the harvest it only
showed that every effort of God's had been wasted on it.
It only produced wild, useless grapes, and there seemed
no answer except to abandon it: 'For the vineyard of the
Lord of hosts is the house of Israel, and the men of Judah
are his pleasant planting; and he looked for justice, but
behold, bloodshed; for righteousness, but behold, a cry'
(Is 5:7). The cry is the wailing of the oppressed.

This image of the vine is one of the most powerful used
by Christ (Jn 15:1–17) to teach the new covenant as a
transformation of human nature through sharing in the
life of Christ, and so sharing in the ultimate love between
the Father and the Son. But this passage from Isaiah is
used more dramatically by Jesus in the parable of the
wicked husbandmen, which he tells to the crowd in the
temple court at the beginning of his last week in Jerusalem (Mt 21:33–46). The parable begins with the same
phrases as the opening of Isaiah's 'song of the vineyard',
and although it is developed in a way which applies it
more directly to Jesus himself as Son of God, the crowd
would recognise the Isaiah passage immediately and
realise that Jesus was making a direct challenge to their
own religious leaders.

In Is 5, the vineyard passage is followed by sections which specify the failures which justify God's abandonment of his vineyard. The nation's leaders and the people, 'the nobility of Jerusalem and her multitude' (5:14), 'call evil good and good evil', they are 'wise in their own eyes and shrewd in their own sight' but they are only outstanding at 'drinking wine, and valiant men in mixing strong drink', and they 'aquit the guilty for a bribe, and deprive the innocent of his right' (5:20–24). This is a rejection of the God who 'shows himself holy in righteousness' (5:16). The holy land will be abandoned to foreigners called by God from the ends of the earth (5:25–30).

1. As christians we believe that we are already living in the messianic age, brought in by Jesus Christ. What evidence could we produce to convey this to our contemporaries? What modern images can be used to convey this belief?

2. What would we accept as modern signs of holiness, in individuals and in the christian church as a whole?

3

The sign of Immanuel
Is 7–8

Is 7:1–14

In 735 BC the long-standing tension between the two Hebrew kingdoms escalated into open war. An army marched on Jerusalem and besieged it, and one of Judah's southern neighbours took advantage of the situation to occupy Judah's sole point of access to the sea, the port of Elath on the Red Sea. There is a terse description of the events in 2 Kings: 'Then Rezin, king of Syria, and Pekah the son of Remaliah, king of Israel, came up to wage war on Jerusalem, and they besieged Ahaz but could not conquer him. At that time the king of Edom recovered Elath for Edom, and drove the men of Judah from Elath; and the Edomites came to Elath, where they dwell to this day' (2 Kgs 16:5–6). The situation has a curiously modern ring to it. King Ahaz of Jerusalem reacted by appealing for help to Assyria, the great Mesopotamian power whose growing strength was reaching into Palestine: 'So Ahaz sent messengers to Tiglath-pileser king of Assyria, saying, "I am your servant and your son. Come up, and rescue me from the hand of the king of Syria and from the hand of the king of Israel, who are attacking me"' (2 Kgs 16:7). Ahaz backed his request with a substantial gift.

Ahaz's action set in train events which were to bring

about the complete destruction of the northern Hebrew
kingdom, Israel, and impose the Assyrian way of life on
Judah for the next hundred and ten years. He was already
notorious for his acceptance of the indigenous Canaanite
religion of Palestine, with its terrible rite of human
sacrifice by burning, and the fertility rites on hills and in
sacred groves, and he had sacrificed his own son to the
Canaanite god Moloch. Isaiah found himself with the
responsibility of guiding Ahaz in this exceptionally
complex international crisis, and Ahaz rejected his
advice.

The crisis was precipitated by the growing power of
Assyria. Palestine was sandwiched between Egypt and
whatever great power had managed to dominate
Mesopotamia. Egypt and the Mesopotamian powers
each thought of the other as the main enemy, so each
sought to control Palestine as its first line of defence; the
Hebrews were living in a potential battle area, and they
were only free from overwhelming external pressure
when both Egypt and Mesopotamia were weak. During
the earlier years of the century Assyria had experienced
such a period of internal weakness, but in 745 BC
Tiglath-pileser set out to regain Assyrian control of
Palestine. The puny kingdoms of Syria and Israel
decided to oppose the growing might of Assyria, and
when Judah refused to join them they opened their
campaign by marching on Jerusalem to force it into an
alliance.

Isaiah approached Ahaz as the king looked down on
the besieging armies from the wall of Jerusalem. King
and people were appalled by the situation: '. . . his heart
and the heart of his people shook as the trees of the forest
shake before the wind' (Is 7:2), for it seemed that the
only choices were between joining the suicidal alliance or

calling to Assyria itself for help. Isaiah told Ahaz that neither of these was the right course; he should sit out the siege and avoid any involvement with Assyria. The besieging army had little chance of taking Jerusalem; Judah should have faith in God and direct its energies to expressing the covenant in the national life rather than becoming involved in international politics.

But Ahaz had already decided to call for Assyrian help, and when Isaiah offered to convince the king with a miracle of Ahaz's own choice, he received a hypocritical reply: 'But Ahaz said, "I will not ask, and I will not put the Lord to the test"' (Is 7:12). The king was set on his disastrous solution to the situation, so Isaiah told him that he would receive a sign whether he wanted it or not, the sign of Immanuel, and it would be a prediction of disaster: 'Is it too little for you to weary men, that you weary my God also? Therefore the Lord himself will give you a sign. Behold, a young woman shall conceive and bear a son, and shall call his name Immanuel (which means 'God is with us'). He shall eat curds and honey when he knows how to refuse the evil and choose the good . . . (before that) the land before whose two kings you are in dread will be deserted' (Is 7:13–16).

We tend to think that words were the only tool used by the prophets, but they also used physical events and actions as symbols to emphasise their message. Isaiah supported his teaching by giving symbolic names to children; thus when he went to Ahaz he named his son 'A remnant shall return' (Shearjashub, Is 7:3) to emphasise the element of hope in his teaching. So now, when Ahaz refused to accept the teaching, Isaiah emphasised God's action and the inevitability of the approaching disaster, by comparing it with the conception, birth and growth of a child. Because Ahaz had refused to recognise God's protecting presence in Jerusalem, and had turned instead to Assyria, God's presence would bring disaster rather than protection. So the child was to be named Immanu-el, 'God is with us' (Is 7:14), and by the time he was old enough to know the difference between right and wrong he would be dependent on curds and wild honey, the food of a nomadic herdsman.

1. The political and international tensions in the old testament are frequently very similar to the problems of today, and the solutions are as disastrous. Is this due to an unchanging and defective human nature? Has nineteen hundred years of christianity made no difference? Is anything in the ancient world worse than the wars of this century?

2. In what ways should—or can—a modern christian influence political and international decisions?

Is 7:14–8:20

Is 7:14b, 'Behold a young woman shall conceive and bear a son, and shall call his name Immanuel', is famous because it is quoted in Matthew 1:22–23 to illuminate the virginal conception of Christ by Mary. We will return to this point at the end of this section, but it should be noted now that there is a real danger of missing the point made by Isaiah if attention is concentrated on Matthew's use of this passage. The Hebrew word translated by 'young woman' refers to a girl of marriageable age, and is not the word normally used of a virgin. Isaiah may have been referring to a normal birth, and in any case the important aspects are the child's name, 'God is with us', and the child's experiences as he grew to manhood. Above all, Isaiah was pointing to the immediate situation and the consequences of Ahaz's decision to call for Assyrian help; he was not suggesting that the only answer to Ahaz's urgent and terrible problem lay more than seven hundred years in the future when Jesus Christ would be born of the Virgin Mary at Bethlehem.

Ahaz's disastrous decision would certainly solve his immediate problem, for the Assyrians would deal decisively with the armies of Syria and Israel which were besieging Jerusalem, but very soon Judah would also be involved in the destruction which Ahaz had unleashed. Immanuel's country would be the front line where the forces of Egypt and Assyria confronted each other, and the settled agricultural economy of the country would be ruined. 'The fly' of Egypt and 'the bee' of Assyria would sweep through the countryside (Is 7:18–19), the Assyrians would shave the people from head to foot (Is 7:20), and 'in that day every place where there used to be a thousand vines, worth a thousand shekels of silver, will become briars and thorns; . . . a place where cattle are let loose and where sheep tread' (Is 7:23–25). The only survivors would be the herdsmen who possessed a cow and a few sheep, who could obtain a meagre living from the milk they gave.

This would be Immanuel's experience. He would grow up in a ruined economy. The people, through their king, had ignored the presence of God and the quiet security and prosperity he would give them if they would concentrate on the way of life he required. They had unleashed the might of the great international powers of their times. To reinforce his point, Isaiah fathered another son, and named him Maher-shalal-hash-baz, 'the spoil speeds, the prey hastes' (Is 8:1–4). The first victims would be Syria and Israel, but the consequences would reach on into Judah. The people of Jerusalem had ignored their God, symbolised by the gentle spring of Gihon whose waters were piped through the conduit of Shiloah to a pool within the city walls (Is 8:6), so 'the waters of the river, mighty and many, the king of Assyria and all his glory' would flood through the land, 'it will overflow and pass on, reaching even to the neck; and its outspread wings will fill the breadth of your land, O Immanu-el' (Is 8:7–8).

The political consequences of Ahaz's appeal came swiftly to Syria and Israel. By 732 BC Damascus had been captured by the Assyrians, and in 721 the northern Hebrew kingdom, Israel, was destroyed. The Hebrews in Israel, whose capital was Samaria, were deported and scattered throughout the Assyrian empire, and their land given to colonists brought in by the Assyrians. The Hebrew hatred for 'Samaritans' dates from this time. Isaiah was mistaken in thinking that the ruin of Judah would occur swiftly, for this did not occur until a century and a half later when the Babylonians destroyed Jerusalem, but Ahaz had created the situation which led to this consequence. The immediate result for Judah was complete subservience to Assyria, with acceptance of the Assyrian religion as the main cult in the temple in Jerusalem (2 Kgs 16:10–16). Isaiah could only call for his teaching to be preserved, 'Bind up the testimony, seal the teaching among my disciples' (Is 8:16), until the times changed. His teaching was to be a main influence on the authors of the book of Deuteronomy, and the reform initiated under its influence by King Josiah a century later, but Isaiah could only see disaster in his own times.

It only remains to discuss the use made of the 'Immanu-el' passage by Matthew. The Greek translation of the old testament, made about 150 BC, used the Greek word for 'virgin' to translate the Hebrew word for 'young girl' in Is 7:14. Matthew used the Greek translation of the old testament, and thus this passage from Isaiah was an obvious one to quote within the context of belief in the virginal conception of Jesus.

If this were all, it would be a weak case for taking this passage as a 'prophecy' of the birth of the Messiah. The meaning of 'Immanuel', God is with us, strengthens the aptness of the quotation, even though it is worth noting that the name occurs nowhere else in the new testament. But the most valuable path of exploration, from this connection between Isaiah's Immanuel and Jesus, is the illumination it throws on the ways in which God's judgement comes into operation. The relationship between God and human beings is established by divine initiative which evokes free human response. It is only by seeing the relationship in these terms that any meaning can be given to mutual 'love' between God and mankind. If the response is not a free one, there is constraint, not love; if the initiative is refused or ignored, the love relationship cannot be completed. This is the basis of all Isaiah's teaching about judgement, and of his forecasts of national disaster. The nation's leaders, and most of the people, have ignored the steadfast faithfulness of God and his continual presence amongst them, so they themselves create their own judgement. The course of action they choose is bound to fail, and its failure will have repercussions throughout their relationship with each other.

This theme runs right through the gospels. People judge themselves by their acceptance or rejection of Jesus: 'God sent the Son into the world, not to condemn the world, but that the world might be saved through him ... And this is the judgement, that the light has come into the world, and men loved darkness rather than light . . .' (Jn 3:17–19). John sets this out clearly in the prologue to his gospel (Jn 1:9–13), but the same theme is worked out in the other gospels as well. In the infancy section of Matthew there is a contrast between Mary, Joseph and the Magi on the one hand, and Herod and his followers on the other. The people for whom the gospels were written were familiar with the context of the old testament quotations to an extent which we have lost, and we must look to the original context if we are to appreciate their full significance. They were sensitive to the consistent pattern of God's relationship with mankind as it is shown throughout the old testament, and they were swift to recognise the fulfilment of this relationship —in all its ramifications—in Jesus.

1. How can the insights of the prophets be applied to times other than their own?

2. In what ways can the pattern of divine initiative and human response be recognised in our own society?

4

Hope for the future
Is 9–12

Is 9:1–20

The dynamics of biblical imagery are created by the human situation in which the images were formed. And they are effective as a continuing force because they continue to focus the experiences of successive generations. Some of the most powerful images in the old testament occur in Is 9–12, and they still speak powerfully to our own times.

The images focus and express the deepest experiences of a generation, and they preserve and transmit it. The images in Isaiah were coined by a Hebrew of the eighth century BC; it is inevitable that they should show their origins, and they certainly cannot be understood unless we are sympathetic towards the situation in which they were formed. Much of the language still awakens echoes in our own experience: the comfort, security and convenience of light and warmth after darkness; the satisfaction of a good harvest; and pride in a nation grown large enough to have no fear of being defeated by an enemy (Is 9:2–3). But some of the images only make sense if the background is known; Is 9:1 refers to the northern part of the country, in the kingdom of Israel, where the Assyrians' advance was first felt as they swept down the great international trade routes which ran through Palestine, 'the way of the sea' which is still the main trunk road through modern Israel. Isaiah felt that the first places occupied by the Assyrians would be the first to experience freedom when God came in glory to liberate them, and Matthew uses this passage to point to the beginnings of the liberation when Jesus the Galilean began his ministry there (Mt 4:12–17), and chose his disciples.

The Assyrian conquest would inevitably awaken memories, central to the national traditions, of the Hebrew situation in Egypt five centuries earlier. The exodus from Egypt was the foundation fact for the Hebrew faith. Whatever it was that actually happened when the Hebrews managed to escape from Egypt, the event had been given fresh layers of significance with every new development in the nation's fortunes. The stories of the exodus were told and retold to successive generations in ways which illuminated their *present* situations, not as mere stories about the remote past with no relevance to the present. The exodus stories were the vehicle of the Hebrew faith as it grew and developed, for the escape was seen as Yahweh's victory over the Egyptian gods, and the people recognised or expected the same kind of victory whenever they were in danger or distress. The power which had brought them out of Egypt, and settled them in Palestine, was the same power which brought them an abundant harvest or which inspired a just decision in the law courts. So Isaiah alludes to the victory over the Midianites during the conquest of Canaan (Jgs 7), as an example of the coming victory (whenever it may come) which will reverse the present calamitous situation (Is 9:4–5).

The present situation had been produced by the disastrous failure of the man who ruled from David's throne in Jerusalem, King Ahaz. In this situation we can see a vitally important development in the Hebrew faith. King David had created the Hebrew state, just as Moses had created the Hebrew people, for he had given the Hebrews their first real security, their first unified government and their first permanent centre of worship. It seemed as if the golden age had arrived, and the guardians of the nation's traditions saw here a new form of the eternal covenant which God had made with the nation at Mount Sinai. So they expected the Davidic line to last for ever, with the kings in Jerusalem acting as God's viceroys (2 Sam 7:8–16). Unfortunately, it had not worked out that way, for the kings had often been the leaders in the nation's flight from God. But the image remained as powerful as ever. God would remain faithful to his choice of the nation. So the people would be saved by God from the consequences of their own apostasy, and there would be an ideal king to lead them back to God again.

Isaiah's confidence in the future is expressed in language which is in stark contrast with the actual kingship as he saw it in Jerusalem. The ideal king ('son of God' is a concept taken from the enthronement rite for a Hebrew king—as in 2 Sam 7:14, 'I will be his father, and he shall be my son', or Ps 2:7, 'He said to me, "You are my son, today I have begotten you . . ."') will be a wonderful counsellor, like Solomon; a godlike hero, like David; and the people will live under him in justice and righteousness and peace, like a family with an ideal father who has the power to achieve what his love desires (Is 9:6–7).

This is an important moment in the development of the Hebrew faith, for it illuminates the situation which generated the concept of a 'messiah', and it marks the end

of an era in the understanding of God's relationship with
his people. The Hebrews of Isaiah's time could point to
four 'proofs' of God's power and of his love for them: the
victories they had won over their enemies; the possession
of the holy land; the continuous succession of kings of the
Davidic dynasty on the throne of Jerusalem; and the
temple with its regular round of sacrifices. They were
beginning to realise that the days of unfailing victory
were over. Now the kingship was being thrown in doubt.
It would survive in increasingly inadequate form (with
two exceptions) for a century and a half, and would end
for ever amidst the ruins of Jerusalem in 587 BC. The
temple would survive until forty years after the death and
resurrection of Jesus Christ, and the holy land is a concept which still has sufficient power to attract pilgrims
and provoke international crises in our own day. But
each of these concepts is, in the end, no more than a
symbol of God's eternal power and love for mankind, and
each symbol can be abandoned when mankind has
grasped the reality which it symbolises. In the messiah,
faith in God began to move from the past to the future.
The old symbols were still used to express this hope, but
there was increasing awareness that the reality is infinitely
greater than the symbols and images by which it is
expressed. Kingship was still the language of faith for
Isaiah, but it was no longer confined to the disillusioning
political institution which controlled the nation's affairs
from David's throne in Jerusalem.

*1. Hebrew historians in the old testament expanded and
adapted the nation's traditions so that they could be applied to
later situations. Do people at all times—including our own—
use history in this way? Is such a process particularly true of
church history? Is it ever 'unbiased'? Could it ever be?*

2. If 'church' is a concept which expresses God's relationship with mankind, what symbols do we use to express and explore this concept? How far are these symbols essential and unchangeable?

In the second half of chapter 9, and the first half of 10, the root causes of the breakdown in the covenant with God are exposed. The first of these is the self-sufficiency of the people, who in their arrogance feel that they can cope with any crisis in the national life, and even produce a better society: 'The bricks have fallen, but we will build with dressed stones; the sycamores have been cut down, but we will put cedars in their place' (Is 9:10). It is a policy of complacency, which expects to create a new and better society without changing the policies and attitudes which have caused the disintegration of the old one. This arrogance is generated and encouraged by the nation's leaders and teachers, 'the elder and honoured man . . . and the prophet who teaches lies' (Is 9:15); but the ordinary people must share in the blame, for they have accepted the teaching and approved of it, so that it has run through the nation like a fire which finds eager fuel. The people cannot evade their responsibilities by laying the blame on their leaders.

The enmity between the two sections of the Hebrew nation, the northern and the southern, is the most blatant sign of the people's failure to respond to the love of God (Is 9:19b–21), but the same disintegration can be seen at a more local level. Unjust decrees, and oppression of the weaker members of the community (the needy, the poor, widows and the fatherless) are symptoms of the same disorder. Far from expecting that the national troubles are only a passing phase which can be reversed, the troubles will increase: '. . . his anger is not turned away and his hand is stretched out still' (Is 9:21; 10:4). 'Anger', when attributed to God, is an obvious anthropomorphism, but it emphasises that the relationship with God is a personal and a moral one in which there is no place for indifference to human complacency and injustice.

Is 10:1–11:16

This complacency in the presence of injustice, and the assumption that God is indifferent to human value, lies behind the condemnation of idols (Is 10:10–11). Under the influence of invasion, and of the people who passed along the international routes which ran through Palestine, the Hebrews accepted elements from many of the neighbouring religions. Some of these were at least modified so that they became useful expressions of the Hebrew faith, but some were starkly incompatible with it. The Canaanite Ba'al cult, with its sacral prostitution and (in some forms) child sacrifice, could never become a way of worshipping the God who had shown his concern for human dignity and justice. The Assyrian astrological religion and the Egyptian cults were less obviously corrupt, but they also failed to make any real connection between the absolute powers and human values or relationships. The multiplicity of gods led to a fragmentation of human relationships and a further separation of religion and social responsibility. The condemnation of idols expresses a more fundamental condemnation of the superficialities of the religions which they represented. The unity of national life, both in its political and its moral aspects, depended on exclusive worship of the one God who is the source of all human desires and abilities.

The Assyrian invasion was the result of political forces,

but Isaiah saw it as a direct result of God's intervention in human affairs to punish the apostasy of his chosen people, even though Assyria does not realise this (Is 10:5–9). This is a crude concept, even when it is used to emphasise the universal power of God, and it is particularly repugnant when it is applied to the appalling cruelty of an Assyrian invasion. Yet there is an element of truth there, for neither the Israelites nor (many years later) the Judeans would have been treated so cruelly if they had not resisted foreign control so strongly, and tried to regain political independence by treachery. Political independence may have been necessary for their religious development in the early period, but that phase had passed, and they were in danger of using religion as a prop for a crude nationalism. The majority of the people still had not realised this at the time of Jesus, and it was a very probable cause of his crucifixion. The kingdom of God as Jesus preached it was incompatible with nationalism, let alone the kind of international supremacy which many of the Hebrews thought their God should give them. But the Assyrians themselves would have to learn this lesson (Is 10:15–19), and in time no great power in the Middle East found itself able to maintain supremacy for very long.

After the long exposition of the approaching disasters and their real causes, Isaiah returns to the themes of survival and hope for the future. The remnant of God's people will realise that 'the Lord, the Holy One of Israel,' is the only true power (Is 10:20–21). The theme of the Davidic messiah, 'a shoot from the stump of Jesse' (Is 11:1), emerges again, to bring in an era of universal righteousness and peace. This will be no mere return to a previous period of Hebrew independence and security; it will be an ideal society in which there is harmony and peace throughout creation, with 'the calf and the lion and the fatling together, and a little child shall lead them' (Is 11:6). If this has echoes of a primitive harmony, such as the compilers of Gen 2:4–19 had so recently depicted, Isaiah takes the ideal far further than anyone before him. Yet the chapter ends with a return to the more practical issues of Isaiah's own immediate world. The exiles would return from the many places where they had been taken; the nation's enemies would be rendered helpless; internal harmony would be restored within the nation; the Davidic empire would be restored and every natural barrier destroyed if they prevented God's people from returning to the holy land (Is 11:10–16).

They are parochial images, but they were effective for the people of Isaiah's time as they groped for the fundamentals of their religion: 'God is my salvation; I will trust, and will not be afraid . . . Shout, and sing for joy, O inhabitant of Zion, for great in your midst is the Holy One of Israel' (Is 12:2–6).

1. To what extent is christianity independent of a particular culture? Should scriptures be more thoroughly 'translated', instead of retaining the images and examples of Hebrew society?

2. What place, if any, is there in modern christian thinking for the idea of punishment by God?

5

The Assyrian attack on Judah
Is 36–39

Is 36:1–37:38

The other part of Isaiah's ministry which can be set against its historical background occurred about 701 BC during the reign of Ahaz's son, Hezekiah. The editor who compiled the Book of Isaiah dealt with this by quoting from the historical book of Kings (Is 36–39 = 2 Kgs 18:13–20:19, with some very significant variations between the two accounts). The material in Is 13–35 is a collection of oracles, which will be considered in the next main section.

Hezekiah is a fascinating figure, for the incidents in his reign are vivid illustrations of the political and religious tightrope which a king of Judah had to walk during the period of Assyrian domination. Once again, the religious experiences and developments in this part of Isaiah cannot be understood if the political situation is ignored. With the destruction of the northern kingdom in 721 BC, the Assyrians established firm control over the whole of Syria and Palestine as far as the border with Egypt. Judah became a puppet kingdom with the Assyrian religion firmly established in the temple and, no doubt, Assyrian agents to keep a careful watch on the country's life.

The Assyrians had good cause for concern, despite

their ruthless suppression of any sign of rebellion. Hezekiah succeeded his father Ahaz to the throne of Jerusalem in 716 BC, and the Assyrian emperor Sargon, who had conquered Israel, was killed in battle in 704. His son Sennacherib succeeded him immediately, but the change in emperor was the signal for risings throughout the empire. From the Babylonians in the far south-east, to the Syrians, Phoenicians and Philistines on the Mediterranean coast, the puppet kingdoms decided that this was their opportunity to regain their independence. The Syrians and Phoenicians both called on the Egyptians for help. The citizens of the Philistine town of Ekron deposed their king when he refused to rebel against the Assyrians and, most significantly, sent him to be imprisoned in Jerusalem. There is no record of an actual rebellion by Hezekiah in Jerusalem, but he was clearly sympathetic towards the Philistines in their bid for freedom.

There had been an earlier incident, before Sargon's death, to show where Hezekiah's hopes lay. Like his northern neighbours, Hezekiah longed for an Egyptian army to march north and take over control of the area from Assyria; in 711 BC Isaiah had gone naked in Jerusalem 'as a sign and a portent against Egypt and Ethiopia; . . . this is what has happened to those in whom we hoped and to whom we fled for help to be delivered from the king of Assyria' (Is 20:3–6). It was an intensely dangerous game for a small nation to play, but all the petty states of the eastern Mediterranean seaboard wove the threads of intrigue and broken alliances as they tested the strength of the great powers which dominated them, and Judah was no exception. Isaiah is the only man known to have warned his people of the dangers, and of the irrelevance of it all to the nation's real welfare.

In 701 the Assyrian emperor, Sennacherib, took an army to the Mediterranean to stamp out the pockets of rebellion. Hezekiah swiftly sent a vast tribute gift of gold and silver stripped from the temple, and a message of complete submission (2 Kgs 18:14–16. This part of the account is omitted in Is 36, because it would spoil the impression of Hebrew superiority over the Assyrians). But the Assyrians still came on to besiege Jerusalem, for the pro-Assyrian king of Ekron was still imprisoned in Jerusalem, and there were strong links between Hezekiah and the rebellious Assyrian province of Babylon. About this time the Babylonians sent an embassy to Jerusalem, and Hezekiah welcomed them with open arms, much to Isaiah's dismay (Is 39). The Assyrians were taking no chances, and intended that Jerusalem and Judah should be eliminated, just as Samaria and Lachish had been destroyed.

The Assyrian general offered terms to the city. Addressing the people in the local dialect rather than the Aramaic of diplomacy, which only the ruling class could speak, he offered a peaceful and prosperous exile if they would submit (Is 36:11; 13–17). There seemed no other choice; the Assyrian general taunted the people with their weakness ('I will give you two thousand horses, if you are able on your part to set riders upon them', Is 36:8), and with the superiority of the Assyrian gods (Is 36:18–20). But the people remained silent, and the king appealed to Isaiah for advice.

Isaiah advised sitting out the siege, despite the terrible example of Lachish, and he predicted that the Assyrians would return to their homeland without taking the city (Is 37:5). The rest of Is 37 shows how this came about: 'And the angel of the Lord went forth, and slew a hundred and eighty-five thousand in the camp of the

Assyrians; . . . Then Sennacherib king of Assyria departed, and went home and dwelt at Nineveh' where, the
account implies, he was swiftly assassinated by his sons
(Is 37:36–38). In cold fact, Sennacherib survived
another twenty years, and the Assyrian records refer to
further heavy tribute exacted from Hezekiah, but it is
also very probable that an outbreak of disease forced the
Assyrians to withdraw from the siege of Jerusalem.

An important and interesting aspect of it all is the way
in which, by modern standards, the bible presents a very
biased account of the events. They are presented as a
clear example of Yahweh's invincible superiority whenever his people trust him; he defeats the Assyrians and
enables his people to gloat over them; once more, as at
the exodus from Egypt, the Hebrews' enemies are driven
back by the Hebrew God (Is 37:22–29). In this case the
background of intrigue and treason shows that the
people had been very uncertain of their God's protective
power, and the events themselves, which left the Hebrews
under clear Assyrian control, could hardly be called a
victory.

*1. Are the motives and actions of the modern great powers and
their dependent states ever any more enlightened than they were in
the ancient world? What are the forces which influence statesmen's
decisions?*

*2. If historical accounts in the bible can be so suspect by
modern standards of historical scholarship and integrity, what is
the nature of biblical 'truth'?*

Is 38:1–39:8

Most of Is 38 is occupied with an account of Hezekiah's
illness, and the cure of it accompanied by a miraculous

sign to convince the king that the cure was really effective. The account is condensed and rearranged from 2 Kgs 20. If the cure was so simple, and so well known— a poultice to drain a boil or an ulcer—it could hardly have needed an Isaiah to prescribe it; so the significance of this passage for an ancient Hebrew is to be found in the 'sign' which Isaiah gave to the king to reassure him, and in the song of thanksgiving attached to it.

The sign in this case is a reversal of the sun's motion, so that a shadow on a set of steps, constructed by Hezekiah to indicate the time of day, moves in the wrong direction. This has no obvious connection with Hezekiah's illness, except that it occurs, as predicted by Isaiah, at the time of the promise that Hezekiah would not die, and so becomes a 'proof' that God will keep his promise.

From our own technological age, it is difficult to project our imaginations into a period when so little was understood of the way in which the natural world behaves. Any event which was 'too hard' for man (the Hebrew root for a 'wonder') could be a 'sign' of God's power, whether it was a political event, such as the escape from Egypt or deliverance from an Assyrian invasion, or an 'impossible' occurrence in the physical world. But there was a steady development in the concept of God's presence and activity, from the idea of occasional divine interventions, to the more subtle and valuable idea of God's universal and continual creative presence which sustains and directs all activity. This sequence of development can be seen by comparing the earlier account of creation in Gen 2:4b–24, and the later account in Gen 1:1–2:4a. When the later position had been reached, the whole natural world and all human relationships could be signs which illuminated God's creative presence, as is shown by the 'wisdom' books, such as Job and Wisdom, which are very late sections of the old testament.

'Signs' take on a further significance in gospels, where every action by Jesus can be seen as a sign pointing to his real character as God incarnate, once his companions are ready to take this point of view about him. But if the people who meet him refuse to consider him in this way, the signs lose their significance and they cannot be convinced. There is no question of making people believe that he is God, against their will. There is hardly an instance (Mk 2:9–12 is a possible exception) in the gospels of a miracle performed to convince people of the divine power in Jesus, and in many cases the miracles are accompanied by commands to remain silent about them. The materials for the gospels were selected and arranged over a period of two generations following the crucifixion, within the experience of the living power of Jesus in the life of the early christian communities. The main events of his life were then presented as signs which came to a focus in the crucifixion and resurrection. On its own, and without this background of belief and experience within a worship-centred christian community, no one miracle or sign could carry conviction. Accepted as a whole, they indicated the range and extent of God's creative power as it was shown by Jesus and experienced by those who accepted him.

The 'song of Hezekiah' in Is 38:9–20 must also be seen as a stage in the developing Hebrew understanding of God's relationship with man. The driving force in this song of thanksgiving is the hopelessness of death: 'For Sheol cannot thank thee, death cannot praise thee; those who go down to the pit cannot hope for thy faithfulness. The living, the living, he thanks thee as I do this day . . .'

(Is 38:18–19). During most of the period of the old testament, and for most of the people throughout the period, the relationship with God ended at death. All rewards and punishments were received during a person's lifetime, it was thought: 'I have been young, and now am old; yet I have not seen the righteous forsaken or his children begging their bread' (Ps 37:25–26); as for the wicked, even though they seem to prosper, 'Truly thou dost set them in slippery places; thou dost make them fall to ruin' (Ps 73:18).

This complacent belief, with its dangerous corollary that the prosperous must be righteous and the unfortunate must all be sinners, began to break during the exile in Babylon when so many of the nation's traditional attitudes went into the melting pot. There is a strand of thought which begins to see death as a force which God will overcome: 'God will ransom my soul from the power of Sheol, for he will receive me' (Ps 49:15). But it was during the persecutions under the Greeks, not two centuries before the birth of Christ, that a firm belief in life after death emerged in such isolated places as the book of Daniel (Dan 12:2) and the histories of the Maccabee rising (2 Mac 7:9, 11, 23; 14:46). It is also significant that this period saw the emergence of the pharisees as a distinct religious group within judaism, for the pharisees believed in the resurrection of the dead while the priestly party, the sadducees, rejected it (Mt 22:23; Acts 23:6–8). The christian belief in the resurrection derives all its force from the resurrection of Jesus, not from any belief inherited from the old testament. For the people of the old testament, death meant descent into Sheol, a place of pale shadowy existence which could only be described in negatives and which contrasted sharply with everything worth living for.

1. Does christian belief depend on the acceptance of miracles, as the older apologetics books used to imagine?

2. Does belief in the resurrection of the dead make any real difference to personal relationships in this life?

6

The collection of oracles and apocalyptic Is 13–35

Is 13–23; 28–35

An ancient author was more often a compiler than an originator. Whoever had a hand in compiling the book of Isaiah, there is clearly much material which cannot be attributed to Isaiah of Jerusalem with any confidence. Yet it is of great interest, for it opens a window onto the attitudes, actions and relationships of ancient peoples throughout the Middle East. The geographical locations covered range from Mesopotamia through to Ethiopia; a distance of more than two thousand miles when it is remembered that the Syrian and Arabian deserts prevented any direct east–west route, and ships were an inefficient and dangerous form of transport.

Babylon, which replaced the ruthless Assyrian empire in 608 BC and destroyed Jerusalem in 587 when the Hebrews finally exhausted its large patience, has a major place in the oracles (Is 13:1–22; 14:22–23; 21:1–10). Most of this material dates from the defeat of the Babylonians, in their turn, by the Persians in 538 BC: 'Fallen, fallen is Babylon; and all the images of her gods he has shattered to the ground' (Is 21:9), and 13:1–22; 14:22–23 stresses the theme of vengeance on Babylon for its arrogance. In point of fact, the exiled Hebrews received very sympathetic treatment by the Babylonians and more of the Jews preferred to remain in Babylonia than returned to rebuild Jerusalem. But the conjunction of nationalism, independent possession of Palestine, and the power of God made the denunciation of Babylon a popular theme. The same theme is more understandable when applied to Assyria (Is 14:24–27), but it is difficult to find any political reasons for the harsh denunciations of the Egyptians and Ethiopians (Is 18:1–19:25), for their power had long been ineffective and the Hebrew kings had looked to Egypt as a saviour from the Mesopotamians. Perhaps this is the key, for the Egyptian alliances had distracted the Hebrews from the priorities of their unique religion, but it is more likely that the poet is looking for any evidence of foreign disaster and attributing it all to the universal power of the Hebrew God.

The minor states which ringed Judah, and which struggled with her to retain a foothold on the narrow strip of the eastern Mediterranean coast, receive no sympathy. By this time the Philistines, who penetrated into the area just after the Hebrews and constituted the first major threat to Hebrew existence, had been conquered and controlled by the Hebrews. Their rejoicing at the Hebrew defeats would turn to lamentation when they in their turn were overrun (Is 14:28–31). The Syrians of Damascus had reaped the fruits of rebellion against Assyria (Is 17:1–6) and never regained their former prominence, but the decline of the Phoenician ports of Tyre and Sidon (Is 23:1–18) was the most remarkable change of fortune: 'Your messengers passed over the sea and were on many waters; your revenue was the grain of Shihor (part of Egypt), the harvest of the Nile; you were the merchant of the nations' (Is 23:2–3). Not only had the Phoenician ships traded with all the known world, including Britain, they had also founded rich colonies throughout the Mediterranean area, from Spain to Cyprus, with Carthage on the African coast as the most famous of them.

To the east of Judah, the Edomites, who had helped the Babylonians to destroy Jerusalem, were natural targets: '. . . all the sighing she has caused I bring to an end' (Is 21:2), and the nomadic Arab tribes whose raids into the cultivated areas of Judah were a constant irritation (Is 21:16–17). But there are two exceptions to the general denunciation and gloating over the defeat of enemies. Some of the Hebrew refugees who had fled into the eastern desert met with hospitality from the nomads: 'In the thickets in Arabia you will lodge, O caravans of Dedanites (a Bedouin tribe). To the thirsty bring water, meet the fugitive with bread' (Is 21:13–14); and the Judeans themselves showed pity and gave help to the Moabites when they were overwhelmed by some unnamed disaster (Is 15:1–16:13).

Much of this is blatant and narrow nationalism to a modern eye, but it is balanced by a condemnation of Judah and Jerusalem, and the Hebrews of the old northern kingdom of Israel, for the same arrogance which led to the fall of the surrounding peoples. To this is added the familiar emphasis on the social evils in Judah and Israel, which are a direct contempt towards the God whom the people worship. The 'rock of Zion' (Is 28:16) is secure for ever, but it is a symbol of the righteous power of God which will destroy the 'covenant with death . . . and your agreement with Sheol' which typifies the national character (Is 28:14–22). The theme runs steadily throughout Is 28–33, the poems against Israel and Judah.

1. Human beings are dependent on social organisation for their very existence, but what kinds of social organisation are essential—and worth defending—in the modern world?

2. How can christianity contribute to the national life in time of war? Can there ever be any justification for blessing weapons? Under what circumstances can religious belief be related to the defeat of an enemy?

Is 24–27

Finally, there are four chapters in the first half of the book of Isaiah, Is 24–27, which belong to that strange and obscure area of religious literature called 'apocalyptic'. The obscurity is deliberate, for apocalyptic emerged at the very end of the old testament period, when the old confidence in God's purposes was eroded by the collapse of the Hebrew monarchy and the fall of Jerusalem. Although Jerusalem was rebuilt together with a new temple to replace Solomon's, and the people gained a foothold on the promised land once more, the monarchy was never restored and it must have been increasingly evident that the Hebrew nation would never be strong enough to defy the great military powers which dominated the Middle East. The Babylonian exile had broken the power of the old symbols of God's supremacy, just because these symbols were derived from a transitory political situation. New symbols emerged, such as wisdom and love, but they would not have the same force as the older ones until they were embodied in the reality which they symbolised, through the incarnation of the Son of God.

In these chapters we can see the first beginnings of apocalyptic, with their note of uncertainty and the hope which cannot be put into very clear images. The reality which surrounds the poet is too vivid to be dismissed with conventional religious confidence: 'From the ends of the earth we hear songs of praise, of glory to the Righteous One. But I say, "I pine away, I pine away. Woe is me! For the treacherous deal treacherously, the treacherous deal very treacherously"' (Is 24:16).

The great prophets of the end of the monarchy and the exile, from Amos to the anonymous second Isaiah, had taught the transformation of society as they knew it. Although their world was corrupt, it was capable of transformation and reform, to evolve a just, contented and peaceful community centred on the worship of God. The apocalyptic writings gain their strength from a thorough disillusionment with all forms of human society, together with an unshakeable confidence in God's determination to impose his will on his creation. So the whole earth must be destroyed to clear the way for a fresh beginning: 'The Lord will lay waste the earth and make it desolate' because 'the earth lies polluted under its inhabitants,' who have 'broken the everlasting covenant' (Is 24:1-5). The disorder is literally universal, for the whole universe is to be involved in the levelling; there is a hint here of the common belief that human affairs are governed by the heavenly bodies: 'On that day the Lord will punish the host of heaven, in heaven, and the kings of the earth, on the earth' (Is 24:21). All power must be subordinated to God.

The result will be a new society in which the people who have remained faithful to God will find their fulfilment; for these are the survivors of the universal catastrophe, the people who have never looked to any power other than God: 'Open the gates, that the righteous nation which keeps faith may enter in. Thou dost keep him in perfect peace, whose mind is stayed on thee, because he trusts in thee . . . O Lord our God, other lords besides thee have ruled over us, but thy name alone we acknowledge' (Is 26:2–3, 13). There is still a strong belief in the place of Jerusalem and the Hebrew nation, purged by punishment and suffering, as the centre of the new society, but there is no longer any clear idea of the political structure which will emerge.

More important still, death will no longer be the ultimate power which removes mankind from its share in God's covenant: 'Thy dead shall live, their bodies shall rise. O dwellers in the dust, awake and sing for joy! For thy dew is a dew of light, and on the land of the shades thou wilt let it fall' (Is 26:19). This will be the final expression of God's universal power. It is not yet seen as a general resurrection of all people, to an eternal destiny of complete fulfilment or complete frustration, but a resurrection of the just and a vindication of God's righteousness: 'He will swallow up death for ever, and the Lord God will wipe away tears from all faces, and the reproach of his people he will take away from all the earth; for the Lord has spoken' (Is 25:8).

When he taught, Jesus Christ had to start from the ideas and images which the people of his time already had. Indeed, as a Jew of the first century AD, they were the vehicles of Christ's own speech and thought; his consciousness of his own personality was expressed in images which he obtained from the community into which he was born. The apocalyptic literature was amongst the most popular and extensive literature available, and its influence can be detected throughout the new testament, particularly in 1 & 2 Thessalonians, Mark 13 and, of course, *the* 'Apocalypse', the Revelation to John. The political situation of Roman persecution, in which the author of Revelation found himself, determines much of the character of that book, but in all new testament apocalyptic there is the same combination: rejection of merely human values and structures, and confidence in a future time when God would triumph and bring the world to the perfect destiny for which he had created it. The details of the imagery are unimportant, provided they convey the essential truths of God's eternally creative power extended to mankind, and the responsibility of man to act in dependence on God so that his power is made effective in love. It may well be that each new generation needs fresh images to supplement the old ones and convey mankind's fundamental relationship with God. The only valid criterion for judging such new images is their effectiveness in expressing the saving truth as it has always been known and expressed by men such as Isaiah, and its supreme fulfilment in Jesus Christ.

1. If apocalyptic was the popular Hebrew literature of Christ's time, what authors are performing a similar function in our own times? Or artists? Or playwrights?

2. If it is always no more than a small minority which responds consciously and effectively to God's love, does this involve 'writing off' most of mankind? Or is the response much wider than formal religious membership would suggest?

Jeremiah
John Challenor

Introduction

The book of Jeremiah as it stands now in the old testament is the 'Jeremiah file', edited by his faithful secretary Baruch, and re-edited by later hands into its present shape. It is a collection of reports of his doings, outlines of his sermons, his comments on the international and domestic situation, letters, speeches, diaries, poems, and prayers—dating over a period of forty years (626–586 BC).

This commentary follows, with a few modifications, the roughly chronological arrangement of the material given it by Baruch and subsequent editors. It follows the text of the Revised Standard Version.

In the absence of modern media of communication, and in the absence of any clear distinction between religion and politics, the output of the old testament prophet was the sort of thing found today not in sermons and religious books only, but in leading articles, controversial periodicals, and television interviews as well. As Jeremiah's thought poured out, it caused great commotions. Most of his contemporaries, if they were not able to laugh it aside, leapt up angrily to refute it, and if possible, to have Jeremiah silenced.

There is every sign that Baruch, who helped Jeremiah and recorded his doings from 609, if not earlier, until both disappear from view after 587, tells the story accurately, without distortion or concealment. It is the story of one of the unhappiest lives possible, if there were no God, and yet at the same time one of the most exciting, full of conflict which ultimately proved fruitful.

The story has perennial interest. Jeremiah lived at a time when vast destructive forces hung over life, erupting from time to time in genocide through deportations, towns reduced to rubble, provinces turned into scorched earth; in fact, in all the scourges represented by the four horsemen of the Apocalypse—invasion, war, famine, and plague (Jer 15; Rev 6).

The story is of particular interest to christians living in the period after the second Vatican Council, for several reasons. Jeremiah was a prophet, and shows us a contribution to the life of the people of God very different from that of the more conventional organisation churchman. He was a member of the (first) people of God, but violently critical of its institutional life. He occupied himself with the task of identifying the true tradition—and consequently of restoring the religious life of Israel—at a time when developments in the Yahweh faith had taken place, so that there was controversy between those who adhered to more recent tradition and those who adhered to a more ancient form. He occupied himself with the problem of public worship and private conversion; with the claims of the social group and the claims of the individual conscience; with public morality in general; and, in a time of war between great and small powers, with the government's foreign policy, and the problem of war and non-resistance. Considering Judah wrong in resisting Babylonia, he found himself forced to decide painfully what loyalty is, and what treason is, in such a situation.

His 'Confessions' show him aware of the darkness that

is often the content of faith—had someone mentioned to him the 'death of God', he would probably have been not altogether baffled. He hit upon the title of the world's best-selling book so far—the new covenant, or new testament (Jer 31:31).

The personality we discover in the book of Jeremiah, and the story that unfolds, are of startling relevance always, but more than ever in the present period of renewal in the churches.

Book list

Here are some of the books drawn upon by this outline, and recommended for further study.

1. *Jerusalem Bible*—text, notes, and introduction.
Studies by A. Gelin, A. Condamin, J. Steinmann, A. C. Welch.
2. The relevant parts of such general books on the OT as
G. von Rad, *Old Testament Theology*, Edinburgh 1965.
B. W. Anderson, *The living World of the Old Testament*, London (2nd edition) 1967.
P. Grelot, *Introduction to the Bible*, London 1967.
R. de Vaux, *Ancient Israel*, London 1961.
John Bright, *History of Israel*, London 1960.
3. The relevant parts of such books on the church, and worship, as
Thierry Maertens, *A Feast in Honour of Yahweh*, London 1966.
Karl Rahner, *The Church and the Sacraments*, London 1963.
Hans Küng, *The Church*, London 1967.

1

The background to the book of Jeremiah

Jeremiah experienced his call to be a spokesman for Yahweh in 626 BC. His complaint that he was only a child (1:6), and too young for the job, suggests he was born not too long before 640. Set out our way, the kings of Judah in whose reigns he lived in Jerusalem are as follows:

Manasseh	687–642
Amon	642–640
Josiah	640–609
(Jehoahaz, for a few months, 609)	
Jehoiakim	609–597
(Jehoiakin, for a few months, 597)	
Zedekiah	597–587

(Fall of Jerusalem, second deportation, and exile, 587)

Jeremiah was born in Anathoth, a village about an hour's walk north of Jerusalem. He was born into a priestly family—that of Abiathar, whom Solomon exiled from Jerusalem to Anathoth and dismissed from the priesthood (1 Kgs 2:27). Jeremiah never functioned as a priest, and he seems to have been brought up in the religious tradition of Sinai, rather than that of Jerusalem.

To explain. By the seventh century, there were two distinct focuses, almost two distinct versions, of the

Jewish faith. One focus was the covenant between Yahweh and his people arising from the escape at the Red Sea, and entered into about 1250 at Sinai through Moses. This covenant required the people to keep the law—the commandments—as the condition of Yahweh's continued favour.

To this original focus another had been added, from the tenth century. As the monarchy was established in Jerusalem, and a unitary kingdom replaced the former twelve-tribe federal structure, a new and up-dated version of the covenant began to be taught. This represented Yahweh as entering into a new agreement with King David, and giving an absolute guarantee of security to David's dynasty, to David's city of Jerusalem, to the temple Solomon would build, and to the mount of Zion on which the city and the temple stood. How, after all, could Yahweh ever allow the temple, where he dwelt, to fall into enemy, pagan hands?

So with the establishment of the united kingdom, about 1000, a rather triumphalist royal theology was born and cultivated within, and side by side with, the older Sinai theology which had prevailed during the desert wanderings, the conquest of Canaan, and the period of the Judges, while the Jews were still organised in a twelve-tribe confederacy. The older form of the covenant tradition can be labelled of Sinai, mosaic, and tribal; and it favoured an egalitarian society. The newer form was of Jerusalem or Zion, davidic, and royal; and it favoured a feudal class-structured society.

How the covenant is understood is crucial, because the covenant constitutes the people of God, and the manner in which the covenant is interpreted and taught governs and conditions the life of the people of God.

The unitary monarchy of Saul, David, and Solomon

lasted less than a century. It split in 922 into two kingdoms, Israel in the north and Judah in the south, and one
important factor in the schism was the fact that the older
tradition was cultivated among the northern tribes, the
newer tradition in Judah. Anathoth, though so near
Jerusalem, lay in the area of the tribe of Benjamin, not
Judah.

A rather important note about names. The people of
Yahweh as a whole throughout their history are *Israel*—
the people of Israel, the descendants of Israel (Jacob)
through his twelve sons, the fathers of the tribes. But this
name 'Israel' was also claimed by the northern kingdom
after 922; the southern kingdom being Judah. The state
of Israel lasted only two centuries. The Assyrians invaded
Israel, took the capital, Samaria, in 721, and deported
most of the population to Nineveh. The Assyrians replaced them with colonists—and it was the descendants
of these gentile colonists, who had mixed with the
residual Israelite population, who were the hated
'Samaritans' of the gospel period. The 'lost ten tribes' of
Israel never returned from their exile. They intermarried
in the east, and ceased to exist as a distinct people. But
Jeremiah was not to know this—in his time, Israel had
fallen a century before, and was a dreadful warning to
Judah. When Jeremiah speaks of Israel, he usually means
the Jewish people of God as a whole. But sometimes
(eg, 3:6) he means the northern kingdom. The context
usually makes it clear. To complicate the matter further,
Israel the northern kingdom is also sometimes called
'Ephraim'.

The social ideas and economic structures of Israel and
Judah can be contrasted as egalitarian and democratic
on the one hand, and proprietorial and capitalistic on the
other. The contrast is too sharp, but the over-simplifica-

tion is useful for making a point which further study can qualify. The Sinai tradition included stress on the equitable division of land, the remission of debts every seventh (sabbatical) year, the freeing after seven years of Hebrews whom poverty had forced into slavery, and the return to owners every fiftieth (jubilee) year of land alienated through misfortune. (For the redemption of land, and the freeing of slaves, see Jer 32 and 34.) These laws were not necessarily at all well observed at any stage, but they express an ideal, equitable division of the goods of the land given by Yahweh to the community as a whole. For a typical protest against violation of this ideal in Israel— by the royal absolutism spreading in from Phoenicia with baalism—see the well-known story of Naboth's vineyard (1 Kgs 21), and the book of Amos.

The Zion tradition was more favourable to proprietory feudalism. Jerusalem had been taken by David while he was still a soldier of fortune and a sort of feudal war-lord. He was a great landed proprietor before being king, and Jerusalem was to some extent his property. The accumulation of property in the hands of a few was more normal in Judah than previously in Israel. Allegiance was claimed by the king personally, not (as in the Sinai tradition) by the tribal elders. Perhaps most significant of all, David introduced the system of forced labour— state slavery—which was the antithesis of the social ideals of the Sinai tradition.

While the northern kingdom of Israel lasted, it was there that the social ideals of the Sinai tradition were cultivated and the innovations of the centralising despotic monarchy were opposed. But in the seventh century, Josiah undertook a 'reformation' in Judah which was an attempt to revive in the southern kingdom the Sinai tradition. Since the reformation was based on the book of

Deuteronomy, it is often known as the deuteronomic reformation. It was while this was going on that Jeremiah received his call.

Jeremiah stands in the Sinai tradition. The eighth-century Isaiah of Jerusalem stands within the Zion tradition. That Jeremiah lived and worked in Jerusalem, and yet taught the themes of the Sinai tradition, is probably due to his origin in Anathoth from a priestly family linked with Shiloh—one of the central sanctuaries where the ark of the covenant was kept, before Jerusalem was even taken from the Canaanites. Jeremiah's preaching of the Sinai tradition in Jerusalem was basically provocative, and was part cause of the friction which was generated between him and the establishment.

Jeremiah's advocacy of the conditional and ethical Sinai tradition, against the Zion tradition which stressed the irrevocability of God's covenant and the value of ceremonial worship, was only one side of his campaign. Another side, simultaneously pursued, was his fight against pagan idolatry—against Judah's joining, in the countryside especially, in the religious observances of the Canaanites.

The horrified language which the prophets use to describe idolatry abounds in the earlier chapters of Jeremiah. There is apostasy from Yahweh on every high hill, and defilement with Baal under every spreading tree. There is adultery, pollution, and prostitution in the worship of abominations—idols—sticks and stones. There is child sacrifice, offering of incense to other gods, and worship of astral bodies and of the 'queen of heaven'.

In these ways Jeremiah refers to native Canaanite and foreign Assyrian practices designed to bring fertility to the soil and prosperity to the inhabitants—rites which easily drew away the people of Israel from their covenant

allegiance to the one, holy, and true God, and his law.
To pass on to the political background. In 626, when
Jeremiah emerged into public life, the little state of
Judah—now, in fact, the whole people of Israel—lay
between 'great powers'. To the south-west lay Egypt;
and to the north-east lay the collapsing Assyrian and
rising Babylonian empires. The decisive year in the north-
east was 612, when the Babylonian leader Nabopolassar
(with help from the Medes) destroyed the Assyrian
capital Nineveh. But from 630 till 612, while the struggle
for power was going on in the north-east, Judah was
relatively free from foreign interference. Good King
Josiah (Jeremiah praises him, 22:15–16) was able
around 630 to shake off the controls imposed by Assyria
—payment of tribute and taxes, and worship of Assyrian
deities in the temple. The year 621 was the climax of a
Judean independence movement. Josiah purged Jerusalem of Assyrian worship. The two previous kings of
Judah, Manasseh and Amon, had been docile vassals of
Assyria, and for as long as living memory stretched back,
Assyrian worship had gone on in Jerusalem. Josiah's
'reformation' was explicitly based on the book of
Deuteronomy, an edition of which was discovered in 621
while the temple was being repaired and decorated and
cleansed of foreign motifs.

The rise to dominance of Babylon, and the fall of
Assyria, were viewed from Egypt with alarm. The
Egyptians decided to prop up the collapsing Assyrians in
order to preserve a counterweight in the balance of
power against Babylonia. So in 609 Pharaoh Neco II
marched north-east to help the Assyrian remnants against
the Babylonians in the upper Euphrates valley. King
Josiah, unwilling to see Egypt and Assyria making
friends and encircling little Judah, intercepted the

Egyptian army as it passed by, at Megiddo. But the Judean force was defeated, and Josiah killed.

This was in 609, so barely twenty years after throwing off Assyrian domination, Judah came under Egyptian domination. Neco at once removed Josiah's heir Jehoahaz (or Shallum) from the throne, and put there another of Josiah's sons, Jehoiakim, who was to pay a heavy tax as Egypt's vassal.

Egyptian control, however, did not last long. In 605, the Babylonians (sometimes called Chaldaeans), under their king Nebuchadnezzar, defeated the Egyptians heavily at Carchemish and chased them back to their natural frontier. And so Judah became subject to Babylon. The mysterious foe from the north of Jeremiah's early chapters comes into sharp clear focus.

Nebuchadnezzar later had to cope with further opposition from Egypt, and about 600 Jehoiakim felt free enough to rebel—he refused to pay the taxes. Nebuchadnezzar marched against Jerusalem. As he approached, Jehoiakim died, probably by assassination, because a disgraceful death is suggested in Jer 22:18.

Jehoiakim was succeeded by his son Jehoiakin (or Jechoniah, or Coniah), who reigned only a few months. Nebuchadnezzar captured Jerusalem in 597, and ordered a deportation of leading men to Babylon. Jehoiakin, most of the leaders and best brains (including the prophet Ezekiel), and most of the available wealth, were transported. Nebuchadnezzar installed as king in Jerusalam Jehoiakin's uncle Zedekiah.

Zedekiah was not strong enough to control the Judean national liberation movement. In 594 unrest in Babylon seemed to be a signal for revolt in Jerusalem; but it got no further than the plotting stage. However in 589, hoping for Egyptian support, Judah did rebel.

Nebuchadnezzar reacted decisively. Jerusalem was besieged. The siege was interrupted briefly when the Egyptians drew off Babylonian troops, but in 587 the city fell. Zedekiah was caught, blinded, and deported. The city, including the temple, was burnt, and its walls knocked down. Many leaders were executed, and another section of the population was deported. So began the exile proper.

The ruins of Judah were added to the Babylonian empire. Gedaliah was made governor of the province. He was assassinated by Jewish nationalists as a collaborator with Babylon. Gedaliah's friends fled to Egypt, taking Jeremiah with them. So ended civilised life in Judah until the restoration organised by Ezra and Nehemiah after the exile. Jeremiah presumably died in Egypt.

The people of the northern kingdom Israel never returned from their exile—her identity was lost. The people of Judah, on the other hand, did maintain their religious life and national identity during fifty years of exile, and were able to return afterwards, and rebuild their national life. Why did Israel disappear, and Judah survive? No doubt historical circumstances favoured Judah. The Babylonians were more humane and tolerant than the Assyrians in their treatment of deportees; and when the Persian king, Cyrus, took Babylon in 539, he positively encouraged the Jews to return to Judah. But one reason for Judah's survival was Jeremiah. His teaching (with that of other prophets) explained intelligibly how Judah could suffer the disaster of exile and yet continue to trust in Yahweh.

Jeremiah is traditionally noted for gloom and pessimism. He is even thought lachrymose, and less than virile. This may be because it was commonly supposed in the past that he wrote the book of Lamentations. Anyone who reads the book of Jeremiah will have this false impression dispelled (as anyone who reads the book of Job will find he was not particularly patient). Jeremiah was a man of quite extraordinary strength and resilience; and his prophecy, when all false hope has been ruthlessly eliminated, is ultimately one of hope—and faith, and love.

1. What were the problems confronting Jeremiah at the outset —within the Jewish tradition, and concerning Israel's relations with the outside world?

2. Why is the term 'Israel' ambiguous? Is there any parallel to the evolution of the term 'Israel' in the evolution of the terms 'church' and 'catholic'? Has the term 'people of God' any advantage from this point of view?

2

Portrait of the prophet as a young man (626–621) Jer 1–6

Jer 1:1–3. The editor gives the book its heading, and introduces Jeremiah.

Jer 1:4–10. Isaiah had become conscious of his vocation in the course of temple worship (Is 6). Jeremiah experienced his (so far as we can tell) in solitude. He puts up a mild resistance, as only a boy yet, and diffident; but his resistance collapses in the face of God's overriding purpose. A share of God's mighty power is passed on to him, to carry out a work both of destruction and of construction, both in Judah and among the surrounding nations.

Jer 1:11–19. No sooner is Jeremiah enlisted as a spokesman for Yahweh than two signs are given him. A look at an almond tree (Hebrew: *sheqed*) brings to him the assurance that Yahweh is watching (the same Hebrew word)—a pun. And secondly he sees on the fire a pot of which the contents are boiling over—towards the south. In this way, it is revealed to Jeremiah that invasion from the north is coming, to punish Judah for her unfaithfulness. (Note that since desert lies to the east of Judah, invasion by eastern neighbours always came from the north, by way of the upper Euphrates).

Jer 2–6. The theme has been stated. Negatively, it is unfaithfulness to the covenant with Yahweh; positively, it is idolatry. Punishment is coming, through the medium of political and military events. Chapters 2–6 are variations on the theme. It is important for us not to look for what is not there—a consecutive, logical exposition. The anthology of poems and sayings actually given us here is better likened to musical development, where a theme is taken up and elaborated and re-stated in different ways, and treated discursively.

Jeremiah follows Hosea in describing the broken relationship between Yahweh and Judah as a broken marriage, wrecked by Judah's adultery—her disgusting worship of Canaanite baals and Assyrian gods. Note that the emphasis in chapters 2–4 is on false worship—and not until chapter 5 on injustice towards neighbours.

Yahweh calls on Judah to return to him. He reminds her that her faithless sister, the northern kingdom Israel, has already been divorced. So far Judah's efforts at self-improvement (3:10)—presumably a reference to King Josiah's reformation—are only skin-deep. What is needed is a real inward conversion—circumcision of the inward heart, not just circumcision of the outward flesh (4:1-4).

From 4:5 to the end of chapter 6 there recur poems on the invasion and destruction of Judah—perhaps the seventh-century BC literary equivalent of Picasso's 'Guernica'.

(4:18) 'Your ways and your doings have brought this upon you.' Together with 2:19, this throws a rather precise light on what may have been Jeremiah's view of the mechanics of divine retribution. Disaster comes, not so much through Yahweh's direct intervention, as by a natural process of cause and effect, through the people's neglect of true worship, the law, and right action . . .

Chapter 5 gives detailed justification for Yahweh's coming ruthless punishment of Judah. 'An appalling and horrible thing has happened in the land' (5:30). Jeremiah lists the sins of injustice against fellow-men in Judah—carelessness about truth; sexual licence; exploitation and impoverishment of neighbours by some who grow 'fat and sleek'.

Chapter 6 gathers up the threads and re-states the theme with a massive crescendo against the city of Jerusalem—a shocking outrage to the official Zion theology. 'Stand by the roads and look, and ask for the ancient paths, where the good way is' (6:16). Jeremiah passes on Yahweh's call for a return to the sources of Israel's faith and true tradition, and for an adjustment to it amounting to a reformation. 'Walk in it, and find rest for your souls.' Here is a piece of the characteristic (rather shallow) deuteronomic theology—obedience will be rewarded by success, prosperity, and peace. But in any case the people have already decided to ignore Yahweh's call. For they have rejected the law (6:19), and the best incense and sacrificial worship offered by those who remain outwardly faithful to Yahweh only displease him (6:20).

Between chapters 6 and 7 some detect a lapse of time. The curtain seems to go up again with chapter 7 as if on a new act—'Jerusalem. Ten years later'. After the first phase of his ministry, it is possible that Jeremiah was forced into retirement or somehow silenced; or that he suffered from severe discouragement; or that he gave himself to study and to the private teaching of disciples. But on the other hand, he himself claims in 605 (25:3) to have been teaching persistently for twenty-three years. (The Jews count part of a year as a year, so from 626 to 605 was twenty-three years to them.) So if there was anything like withdrawal after 621, perhaps it was only a relative one.

1. *How did Jeremiah's home and family background affect his teaching? Can you see any significance, possibly, in the fact that Jeremiah's call is not described as taking place at temple worship (as Isaiah's is)?*

2. *Is the marriage bond really helpful as an analogy to illustrate God's relationship with his people? (See 13:11 for another arresting physical analogy.)*

3. *Is it possible to say how Jeremiah saw the relationship between false worship and injustice to neighbour? Are they wholly distinct; or exactly identical; or somehow interrelated? (The relation of theory and practice may be a helpful analogy.)*

4. *Is the situation Jeremiah describes irretrievable? Is disaster certain? Or is repentance still a possibility? (See 4:14; 6:8.)*

3

The temple sermon of 609 and the reign of Jehoiakim Jer 7; 26 and 8–20

Jer 7:1–8:3 and 26. In 609, at the beginning of Jehoiakim's reign, on a day of harvest festival when the courtyard of the temple was crowded, Jeremiah addressed the people. For what he said, he was seized and brought to trial. He told the people not to place any trust in the temple (7:4). He prophesied against the temple and against Jerusalem. He was accused of blasphemy—of denying the dogma of the inviolability of Zion. It was a case not unlike that of Stephen (Acts 6) and even of our Lord (Mk 14:58; Jn 2:18–22). Christ quotes Jeremiah's description of the temple as a robbers' den at Mk 11:17.

King Josiah was killed at the battle of Megiddo in 609. A son, Jehoahaz, reigned for a few months. The Egyptians (victors at Megiddo) removed him and placed on the throne another of Josiah's sons, Jehoiakim. With him, all hope of Josiah's reformation getting anywhere evaporated.

It was at the beginning of Jehoiakim's reign that Jeremiah spoke out. Two accounts of his sermon were preserved in the Jeremiah file, one as given by Jeremiah himself (Jer 7), and the other as narrated by his secretary Baruch (Jer 26). (Jer 26–45 are Baruch's biographical memoirs of Jeremiah's life.)

Jeremiah denounced the arrogant complacency of

133

official Judah, which regarded the temple and Jerusalem as such a firm and unconditional guarantee of Yahweh's favour and protection that there was no need to be over-anxious about true worship and right action. So dreadful things were going on—worship of the Assyrian fertility goddess (7:18), child sacrifice (7:31), contempt of all the commandments (7:9). In fact, the imagined security of Jerusalem is a dangerous delusion (7:4), and the temple will suffer the same fate as the Shiloh sanctuary before it. (Shiloh was destroyed by the Philistines about 1050; the ark of the covenant was taken, and kept some time in enemy hands; returned later, it was set up by David in the tent, then by Solomon in the temple, at Jerusalem.)

As Jeremiah finished speaking, a lynching seemed possible (26:9), when the temple authorities arrested him. He was charged with seditious blasphemy, but acquitted. The family of Shaphan, one of the king's ministers, defended him. And some elders argued that the destruction of Jerusalem had already been prophesied around 700 by Micah (3:12), who got away with it. Jeremiah's words were within the orthodox prophetic tradition. So Jeremiah 'was not given over to the people to be put to death'. (He *did* have some friends.) But to show how near to violent death he came, Baruch tells the story (26:20–24) of the prophet Uriah, who taught what Jeremiah taught, and who was executed under Jehoiakim.

A note on 7:22. The detailed rules about animal holocaust (burnt offering) and sacrifice which are found now in the Pentateuch were not there in Jeremiah's time—they were probably added during or after the exile. The law in Jeremiah's time emphasised the ethical code of the commandments, and it suits Jeremiah's purpose to point this out. Some animal sacrifice was certainly practised in the period of the desert wanderings—the passover, for example. But, as Fr de Vaux points out, Jeremiah is not writing a critical scientific history of Israelite sacrifice for theology students; he is preaching against externalism, and for inward conversion of heart, to the people as a whole. It is important to interpret Jeremiah's sayings in their context. He is not revealing nuggets of timeless truth for us to dig out and re-set as foundation stones in dogmatic textbooks. He is appealing to hearts and minds for the appropriate response to Yahweh's declaration of love.

Jer 8:4–10:25. More variations on the main theme.

Jer 11:1–17. Jeremiah had supported the reformation directed by king Josiah. He had volunteered to help as a street-preacher (11:6), reminding the Judeans of the Sinai covenant and trying to elicit the response of faith. In 11:9–17 there is a reflection of Jeremiah's disappointment and disillusionment with a movement which changed nothing below the surface. He returns to attack temple worship (11:15).

Jer 11:18–23 and 12:6. Here is a piece of evidence that Jeremiah favoured the reformation movement of Josiah. One provision of that reform was that all worship should be centralised in Jerusalem. The provincial shrines, or 'high places' were to be closed down, so that a careful vigilance could more easily ensure the future purity of Israel's worship—uncontaminated by the infiltration of Canaanite practices in the countryside.

But a revealing verse (2 Kgs 23:9) tells us that this legislation, which would have caused unemployment and redundancy among the country priests, was not observed. This is the context of Jer 11:18–23. Jeremiah's own priestly family at Anathoth conspired to kill him, almost certainly because he was supporting the reformation which threatened their livelihood. But in general though Jeremiah admired King Josiah (22:15) he found little joy in the king's reformation. There was increase of cultic activity without corresponding amendment of life.

In 8:8–9, we glimpse the conflict Jeremiah was in. It was obviously good that the old covenant should be restored. But once restored, it could be its own worst enemy, in making the people feel satisfied. The same imagined inviolable security conferred by the davidic covenant (as interpreted by the popular national theology) could be arrived at by a different route— through the Sinai covenant. So the people again became deaf to the voice of Yahweh and his prophets (8:9). It was just as dangerous to have a delusory security based on a book as one based on a building.

Jer 12:1–6. This plot against Jeremiah's life—'Let us destroy the tree with its fruit' (11:19)—is the occasion for a complaint to God. 'Why does the way of the wicked prosper?' Jeremiah raises a question of the mystery of evil, later raised by Job and in the wisdom books of the old testament. Yahweh's astringent reply is to the effect that Jeremiah's sufferings have not really begun yet . . .

This complaint, a prayer in the style of some of the psalms, is one of several. Notice others in chapters 15, 17, 18, 20. They are usually labelled the 'Confessions' of Jeremiah. There is a note about them on p. 138–9.

Jer 13:1–11. Taken literally, this story involves huge and improbable journeys. It may be an interior vision, objectivised. Or the 'Euphrates' may be a mistranslation, and a stream near Anathoth may be meant. If the latter is the case, then this is an 'acted parable'. It is clear anyway that the deterioration of the loincloth signifies the deterioration of Judah through idolatry. (To see why Judah is like a loincloth, read 13:11.)

Jer 14–15. Variations on the theme. Note the 'Confession' in 15:10–21.

Jer 16. As a sign to the people of impending disaster, Jeremiah is instructed to remain unmarried and childless; and even to avoid all sociable gatherings, whether for mourning or for rejoicing. So 'I sat alone'—'I held myself aloof' (15:17). In this way, Jeremiah's whole style of life became an acted parable. Celibacy was very unusual in Israel.

Jer 17. The passages on the temple and the sabbath are quite uncharacteristic of Jeremiah, and may be later interpolations into the book.

Jer 18:1–12. Jeremiah was called to be a destroyer and a creator (1:10). What he saw done in the potter's workshop revealed to him Yahweh's design to destroy the existing Judah and (through the exile) create a new people, with a new covenant. From this starting-point, Jeremiah was able to give an intelligible theological explanation of the national disaster before it happened, so as to help make it possible for Judah's faith to survive.

Jer 18:18–23. Another 'Confession' in which Jeremiah reacts fiercely to another plot.

Jer 19. Having realised a truth in the potter's workshop Jeremiah proceeds to a demonstration. First, before a chosen audience of priests and elders, he breaks a jug, and expounds the meaning of the symbolic action. Then he repeats his message to the people at the temple.

Jer 20. For this he is arrested by the temple authorities, beaten, and put in the stocks for a night. This was about 605.

Jer 20:7–18. Another 'Confession'. This a point at which to consider the 'Confessions' as a whole (11:18–12:6; 15:10–21; 17:14–18; 18:18–23; 20:7–18). They are private prayers, wrestling encounters with God. Jeremiah had resisted his call at the beginning. As difficulties increased, he resisted again and again. He took Yahweh's side against the people; then, ill-treated by the people, he felt deserted by Yahweh, and terribly alone. He accuses Yahweh of seducing him (20:7), and of being deceptive and changeable like a Judean stream, a full torrent at the time of the rains, then suddenly parched all summer (15:18). He curses the day he was born (20:14).

These confessions all express a distress at the darkness which shrouds Yahweh and makes his will a mystery. Jeremiah strips off everything pertaining to appearances and reason and nature, and holds on in darkness and seeming failure, by faith.

In this way, there grows in Jeremiah a more personal faith with a very strong root. The French scholar Albert Gelin makes the following points about Jeremiah and 'personal religion'. Until Jeremiah and the exile, the faith of Israel was the faith of a group. But with Jeremiah and the exile there emerged a new phenomenon, the *anawim*, the poor of Yahweh, who through the tension of suffering and failure are led into closer personal relationship with God. For Israel until Jeremiah, religion and the national life were one. Since Jerusalem was destroyed in 587, and the national life brought to an end, there would have been a danger—but for Jeremiah's new spirituality—of the collapse and extinction of the faith. In fact, in exile, the community reformed itself, without temple or national life, upon the new principle of the inward obedience and commitment of individuals. Not only did Jeremiah help Israel survive in this way; he also passed on this principle as the religious programme of the future—the new covenant. Not accepted in his lifetime, after his flight into Egypt and his death Jeremiah exercised a profound influence upon the exiles and Jewish tradition.

1. *What was Jeremiah's attitude to the temple, and temple worship? Examine the part of buildings in the life of the Jewish and christian peoples of God. (See Gen 28: 17; Jn 2: 21; Acts 6: 13; 1 Pet 2: 5).*

2. *Has Jeremiah's critique of triumphalism anything to say to us in the church today?*

3. *What was Jeremiah's attitude to Josiah's reforming programme?*

4. *Are vested interests like those Jeremiah collided with (11: 18–12: 6) a harmful brake on needed renewal, or a valuable brake on superficial change?*

5. *'You must not take a wife' (16: 2). What is to be said about refraining from marriage and childbearing in difficult times? Did it render Jeremiah more free? Was it a valid sign? (See 1 Cor 7; cf J. H. Newman, Apologia, where he says 'another deep imagination . . . took possession of me . . .(at the age of 16) . . . that it would be the will of God that I should lead a single life'. Cf also the 'three postponements' proclaimed by the government of North Vietnam in 1967: 'postpone falling in love; postpone marriage; postpone having children—until the end of the war'.)*

6. *Can we quote Jeremiah to legitimise protest demonstrations, marches for peace and civil rights, etc?*

7. *What light do the 'Confessions' throw on the relationship of*

Jeremiah with God, whether as individual or prophet—is there a difference?

8. Would Jeremiah have understood the modern phrase 'the death of God'?

9. Does Jeremiah exhibit the virtue of abandonment to the will of God? Was he naturally submissive and resigned?

10. Ought we to be always polite and respectful in our converse with God?

11. Was Jeremiah really as friendless and deserted as he sometimes makes out?

12. Jeremiah showed that the way to the renewal of the shallow religion of the nation of Israel was by way of the conversion and commitment in deep faith of a relatively small number of individuals. Has this teaching any relevance for the church today?

4

The publication of the prophecies (605), and the reign of Zedekiah
Jer 36 and 25:1–13; 22–24 and 27–29

Jer 36. One further incident from the reign of Jehoiakim. It is still 605. Jeremiah is banned from the temple (36:5), and therefore sends Baruch to read Yahweh's message to the people. He dictates a scroll to Baruch, and Baruch goes to the temple and reads it from a window overlooking the courtyard.

The incident is reported to the king's ministers. The cabinet summons Baruch, and hears that Jeremiah is the author of the scroll. Unexpectedly sympathetic, they advise Jeremiah and Baruch to go into hiding; and the officials take the scroll to the king.

It is winter, and Jehoiakim is sitting by a fire. As the scroll is read out to him, he cuts off pieces with his knife and throws them into the fire with a jaunty nonchalance that would have infuriated Jeremiah. The reading finished, and the scroll burnt, the king orders the arrest of Jeremiah and Baruch.

From hiding Jeremiah hurls back the assertion that Jehoiakim will die a disgraceful death. Meanwhile he hands Baruch a fresh scroll and proceeds to dictate a new, enlarged, and revised edition of his prophecies.

We do not know exactly what the scroll burnt by Jehoiakim contained. The government's alarm suggests that the message was explicitly political—probably a rather precise threat of Babylonian invasion and of exile, if Jer 25:1–13 are any guide. This would be extremely annoying to Jehoiakim because in 605 he had just been forced, after the battle at Carchemish when Babylonia defeated Egypt, to sign a treaty with Nebuchadnezzar as a tax-paying vassal, or subject king.

Jer 22–24. In 598 Nebuchadnezzar marched on Jerusalem to deal with the insubordinate Jehoiakim. The story is told in 2 Kgs 24. Jehoiakim died, probably murdered. Jehoiakin (Jechoniah, Coniah) ruled briefly in his place, till the Babylonians arrived. Nebuchadnezzar ordered the deportation of the leaders, including Jehoiakin, and installed the more compliant Zedekiah as king over those too undistinguished to be worth deporting. (Numbers deported are variously estimated, from 3,000 to 10,000. The population of Judah may have been 120,000.) Zedekiah, already weak by nature, was weaker still because many insisted on recognising Jehoiakin as the legitimate king.

Jer 22. This a chapter of pithy comments on four kings of Judah, who are judged by the criterion of their faithfulness to the Sinai covenant. Only Josiah passes the test. Notice the contrast between Jehoiakim, who self-indulgently builds himself a vermilion palace by forced labour, and Josiah, who 'did justice and righteousness', and 'judged the cause of the poor and needy'. 'Is not this to know me? says the Lord.'

Jer 23:1–8. Disgusted with the present useless shepherds —kings—Yahweh will in days to come raise up a good king. He will anoint a virtuous descendant of David—a messiah.

Jer 24. The vision of the two baskets of figs is unusual for Jeremiah in that it is related to the temple. The good figs stand for the exiles, about whom Yahweh uses the language of the new covenant. The bad figs stand for the population left in Judah—Zedekiah and his subjects. The exiles are the seed of the future, re-created Israel; the remnants left in Judah are rejected.

Jer 29. Jeremiah wrote to the exiles in Babylon. He advised them to settle down, build houses, plant gardens, marry, and raise families. The future is hopeful. Yahweh will repatriate them, though only after a long exile. (Seventy years is a term for a long period. In fact the exile lasted fifty.) Jeremiah denounces by name certain misleading prophets, who were advising active resistance to the Babylonian authorities. One of the exiles in turn denounces Jeremiah as a false prophet, a madman, who ought to be put in the stocks and iron collar. Jeremiah replies that his accuser will die without male descendants.

The problem of false prophets is now a burning issue. Jeremiah had many enemies—priests, people, government; even Yahweh, he sometimes felt, was not with him. Now hostility breaks out from another quarter—the false prophets.

Jer 27. Around 594 Egypt stirred up to revolt against Babylonia, Judah's small neighbours—Edom, Moab, Ammon, Tyre, and Sidon (roughly, the modern Jordan and Lebanon). Judah was pressed to join the coalition.

Jeremiah made a yoke, with thongs, and wore it as a sign that Judah should not join the revolt but should remain in subjection to Babylon. He warned Judah, and

through their envoys in Jerusalem warned the surrounding nations, to submit to the facts of history, and
not to listen to the false prophets who with facile optimism were counselling revolt.

Jeremiah, wearing his yoke, counselled submission, not
for love of Babylon, nor for political advantage, but
because Yahweh was using Nebuchadnezzar as his
servant (27:6) to bring good out of evil for Judah.
Through the exiles in Babylon, God was building and
planting (29:5; 1:10).

Jer 28. Jeremiah had an altercation with a false prophet
Hananiah, one of the easy optimists popular with the
patriots and nationalists. Hananiah prophesied the
return of the exiles within two years. Jeremiah, still
wearing the yoke, argued that the true prophets had
always prophesied disaster—because the people had
always been unfaithful. If a so-called prophet diverged
from the tradition, the onus of proof was on him to justify
himself. If he could not, he was false. The furious Hananiah seized the yoke off Jeremiah's shoulders and broke it.
Jeremiah asked what he would do with a yoke of iron,
and prophesied Hananiah's death. Within two months
Hananiah was dead (28:1, 17).

Jer 23:9–40. Here is a tirade against false prophets.
23:17 repeats the point—those who prophesy peace for
the wicked and good fortune for sinners, are obviously
wrong and wicked. How could this be the will of Yahweh?
23:18 throws light on the question how the prophet
knows the word and will of God.

*1. Why was Jeremiah taken so seriously by the government?
Why was he subject to censorship? Does his life throw any light
on our modern problems of censorship?*

2. In his praise of King Josiah (*22 : 15–16*), how far does Jeremiah equate love of God and love of man? Has he a place for direct prayer to, and worship of, God? (*Cf J. A. T. Robinson,* Honest to God, *60, where he explains this passage to show that 'God, since he is Love, is encountered in his fullness only "between man and man"'. See also Jer 9 : 23–4; and the 'Confessions'.*)

3. Why was Jeremiah's teaching on the good and bad figs so offensive to Zedekiah and the court prophets?

4. Jeremiah recommends submission to Nebuchadnezzar, Yahweh's servant (*27 : 6*), and tells the exiles to work for the good of Babylon (*29 : 6*). What light is thrown here on the relationship between the people of God and the rest of the world?

5. How does Jeremiah's advice to the first exiles to 'take wives . . .' (*29 : 5*) square with his own single state?

6. What were Jeremiah's main criteria for distinguishing true from false prophecy? John XXIII, in his opening speech at Vatican II, disagreed with 'those prophets of gloom, who are always forecasting disaster'. Was he not, according to Jeremiah's standards, a false prophet?

5

The siege and fall of Jerusalem (588–587) Jer 21; 32–35; 37–45

Jer 21. In 588, as Nebuchadnezzar advanced on Jerusalem a second time, but before the siege closed in, Zedekiah sent another Pashur (not the one who had Jeremiah beaten, 20:1) to ask if there was any hopeful word from Yahweh. Probably Zedekiah was hoping for a repetition of the wonderful deliverance of Jerusalem in Isaiah's time, when Sennacherib and the Assyrian besiegers suddenly and for no obvious reason broke off the siege and withdrew homewards, strengthening dramatically the popular belief in the inviolability of Zion (2 Kgs 19).

Jeremiah's answer was as stark and trenchant as usual. The siege will close in; Yahweh is with Babylon, to destroy his unfaithful people; the king will die; the only way to save one's life is to surrender to the Babylonians.

Jer 34:1–7. Jeremiah spells out the answer of chapter 21 in more detail.

Jer 34:8–22. Hoping to gain Yahweh's favour, Zedekiah announces a reform. The Sinai law forbade a Jew to enslave a fellow-Jew. The government accordingly decreed the release of Jewish slaves. The reform was

decreed with religious ritual—the sacrifice of a calf—but
was probably motivated by self-interest. Shortage of food
as the siege tightened, and the need for more fighting
men, made it opportune for the possessing classes to cut
down their households. Then conditions temporarily
improved, the siege was partially lifted (34:22) and the
slaves were promptly re-enslaved (34:11).

Jer 32:1–15. Jeremiah is now in prison for spreading
alarm and despondency and advising desertion in a time
of national emergency. The siege is being pressed again
(32:24) and enemy earthworks are moving nearer to the
city. To the royal prison comes a cousin of Jeremiah from
Anathoth offering him as a member of the family the
option to buy back a field there, according to the law of
redemption (Lev 25:25).

Anathoth was enemy-occupied territory. Jerusalem
was closely encircled. Famine was already claiming
victims. At that moment, Jeremiah dramatised his faith
in the future restoration by solemnly buying the field in
due legal form for a fair price; 'Houses and fields
and vineyards shall again be bought in this land'
(32:15).

Jer 32:16–44. A prayer, containing a summary of the
teaching of Jeremiah as a whole. The hopeful promise
made to the exiles (24; 29) is repeated.

Jer 33. Amplifies the promises of 32; but the second half
of chapter 33 is not by Jeremiah—it is a later addition by
a writer in the Jerusalem covenant tradition.

Jer 35. The ultra-conservative Rechabite clan of nomads
who normally insisted on living in tents away from built-
up areas and civilisation, had taken refuge in Jerusalem.

Jeremiah makes them the occasion of a prophecy—he commends their careful faithfulness to their founder, and regrets that Judah cannot show a similar faithfulness to her tradition.

Jer 37. Egyptian troop movements caused the Babylonians (or Chaldaeans) to raise the siege temporarily. Jeremiah still holds out no hope to Zedekiah: the siege will be resumed, and the city will fall. But while the siege was interrupted, Jeremiah decided to return to Anathoth to his family (either he had been released or chapter 37 narrates events previous to chapter 32). Leaving the city, he was arrested as a deserter, beaten, and imprisoned, first in a dungeon, and then in the royal prison.

Jer 38. But his enemies, the more warlike and hawkish of the leading Judeans, insisted that the king put him to death for subversion and treason. Zedekiah caved in to their pressure. Jeremiah was thrown into a well in which was only mud, and left to starve. But a Cushite (Ethiopian) servant of the king rescued Jeremiah, and returned him to the royal prison. In another private interview with Zedekiah, Jeremiah again counselled him to surrender.

Jer 39. The harrowing record of the fall of Jerusalem is told here, and also in 2 Kgs 25, and again in Jer 52—as a conclusion to the book as a whole. The burning of the temple is recorded in two of the accounts. Zedekiah was caught and rendered powerless for the future by being blinded.

On Nebuchadnezzar's orders, Jeremiah was released from prison and given protection by the victors. So anyway says 29:11–14. 40:1–6 shows him being released at

Ramah, the assembly-point from which the chained deportees were marched to Babylon. The confusion of the time is mirrored in the confusion of the narrative. He was allowed to choose for himself where to go.

Jer 40–45. After the destruction of Jerusalem, Jeremiah chose to join Gedaliah, who was left in charge to govern the remains of Judah, from Mizpah. But Jewish nationalists assassinated Gedaliah as a collaborator with Babylon. Jeremiah and Baruch wished to stay in Judah (42), but their friends, fearing Babylonian reprisals, insisted on taking them to Egypt. In Egypt, Jeremiah continued indefatigably reprimanding the emigrant Jews for their false worship (44); and he prophesied disaster for the Pharaoh (43). Jeremiah presumably died in Egypt: but there is no record of his death.

The section closes with a word of encouragement for Baruch, personally, spoken in the crisis of 605, but placed here by Baruch as a conclusion to his biography of Jeremiah. Jeremiah remembered his friends—the Ethiopian who saved his life also got a reassurance (39: 15–18).

1. How does Jeremiah's purchase of land as Jerusalem was falling in 587 square with his earlier withdrawal from marriage and social life? Was he getting more hopeful as the situation got worse?

2. How does Jeremiah's experience illustrate the difficulty of reconciling conflicting loyalties? (Or the problem of conscience and authority.) Is the difficulty increased where the people of God, and the state, coincide?

3. Is there any evidence that Jeremiah ever considered formally separating himself from the people of God? Was it a thinkable possibility?

4. *Has Jeremiah anything to say to those contemporary christians who believe, but are put off by the 'organisation'?*

5. *What sort of a man was Baruch?*

6. *Since Jeremiah believed Israel's future lay with the exiles (24), why did he not take the opportunity of joining them after 587?*

6

The new covenant
Jer 30 and 31

This 'book of consolation', as it has been called, is in two parts.

Jer 30 and 31:1–22

This part dates from the reign of Josiah, who died in 609. In his last years, Assyria was collapsing, Judah was re-taking the land from which northern Israel had been deported, and there was optimism about Israel's restoraation. 'Ephraim, my first-born son' is to return—so, no more weeping at Ramah. (Rachel, Jacob's wife, and so the mother in a way of all Israel, is pictured weeping at Ramah, which was her burial place and also an assembly-point whence deportees were marched east. Mt 2:18 uses this reference as a foretelling of the massacre of the innocents.)

Jer 31:23–40.

This second part of the section is the theological heart of the book of Jeremiah. It probably dates from 587, and it deals with the restoration of Judah.

The question arises, if the restoration of Israel never happened, and the hopes in 30:1–31:22 were never ful-

filled, why should we take the second half of 31 seriously?
The answer seems to be that the prophesied restoration of
Judah *did* take place, so that great value came to be set on
this section.

The restoration would be possible because the old rule
of collective responsibility condemning the innocent with
the guilty will no longer hold. Reward and punishment
will be individualised, so that a minority of repentant
faithful will not be for ever dragged down in judgement
by the unfaithful majority; but they will be the new seed
from which the new people will grow.

The official national theology of Judah was based on
Yahweh's word through Nathan promising security to
David's line and to Zion (2 Sam 7). Yet in 597 Zion fell
and the king went, a prisoner, to Babylon; and when the
more drastic blow fell in 587 the state theology was left in
ruins. Here was a theological contradiction of the first
order—Yahweh had broken his promise. Some questioned
Yahweh's power; others doubted his fidelity. Perhaps
after all other gods had more to offer. The factor in the
equation so far omitted, but brought in insistently by
Jeremiah, was the sin of the people. Jeremiah was able to
demonstrate that the fall of Judah was a just judgement
of the faithful all-powerful Yahweh. And since the explanation was in terms of the people's sin, it already pointed
the way to future restoration—through repentance.

The question arises, was Jeremiah a pioneer of individual religion and personal responsibility—as against
'primitive' unthinking collectivism in religion? Jeremiah
looked forward to a new community based on individual
commitment. He did not stand for an individualist faith
though in the circumstances of a collapsing national cult
he was forced into a rather individualistic position, in
order to proclaim to other repentant individuals the hope

of a new community in the future. For Jeremiah was as unacceptable to the defenders of the official national cult as that cult was to him.

For fifty years in Babylon the Jews had no temple, no public sacrificial worship, no land of their own. Ordinarily, the gradual evaporation of the Yahweh faith might have been foreseen. That this was not the outcome was partly due to Jeremiah's stress on the internal personal side of faith—the production in a faithful minority of a religion of the heart strong enough to issue in new social forms of faith. And because of its emancipation from a particular land, city and temple, and from a particular local culture, this 'religion of the heart' had within it the potentiality of being universal.

From his brief remarks on individual responsibility, Jeremiah moves on quickly to the community, to the new covenant and the new people (31:31–34). Already the theme of the new covenant has been heard, in Jeremiah's occasional teaching: in 24:7 when he addresses the exiles, and 32:37 when he explains his extraordinary behaviour over the field he bought when Jerusalem was falling.

The old covenant had lapsed. Not from God's side, of course, because God is faithful, dependable, and sure. This unshakable dependability is one of God's most obvious characteristics, as Israel knew him. Nor is the old covenant out-dated. It is simply that Israel had broken it by her disobedience and non-observance. The failure of Josiah's reform was the last straw.

So God again takes the initiative and announces a new covenant. The Hebrew *berith*, covenant, became the Greek *diathēkē*, the Latin *testamentum*, and the English 'testament'. The term 'covenant', connoting an agreement between two fairly equal partners, was transposed as soon as the Hebrew scriptures were put into Greek,

into the term *diathēkē*, 'testament', which connotes the
gift ('will and testament') of God, coming to man, who in
his subordinate place receives and responds.

Jeremiah's words on the new covenant profoundly
influenced later prophetic tradition, and were taken up
by Jesus himself. In a way, Jer 31:31 is the great inter-
section or cross-roads at which all the traffic of the old
testament from the exodus onwards converges, and
diverges again in the direction of the last supper and the
new testament. Jeremiah preaches the Sinai covenant,
takes up the earlier prophetic teaching, uses here and
there the style and themes of the wisdom literature, and
takes up the davidic messiah theme (23:5–6). And all
this he re-orients towards the future with a new stress on
redemptive suffering.

But if 'the gifts and the call of God are irrevocable'
(Rom 11:29), how can there be a *new* covenant? The
new covenant is new in so far as it will fulfil the original
purpose of the old, Sinai, covenant. What is new is the
means, even more than the content. God will change the
heart of man, to make it receptive. It is not simply that
man will progress from obeying external commands,
passed on through Moses, to obeying internally from the
heart. This latter is what Deuteronomy was already
asking of Israel (Deut 6:4–6). Jeremiah goes further, and
envisages a change which remakes man in such a way as
to enable him to overcome all duality between God's will
and his own. In other words, he will really love God—his
will and God's will coincide. Jeremiah locates this in the
future—'the days are coming'. The new covenant
belongs to the last days, the age to come, the kingdom of
God.

Other prophets speak of the new covenant in terms of
the Spirit of God being poured out—see Joel 2:28,

quoted in Acts 2:17. Others, again, speak of violent apocalyptic changes in the cosmic order and in the natural order on earth. But Jeremiah speaks mildly of a happy resumption of ordinary family and religious life—rejoicing in the rebuilt villages, 30:19; and pilgrimages to Jerusalem, 31:6. For Jeremiah, the change is not some great cataclysm in the cosmic order, but something within men's hearts. It is still a colossal transformation, because left to itself 'the heart is deceitful above all things, and desperately corrupt' (Jer 17:9).

'And I will be their God, and they shall be my people' (31:33). These words, and the following verse 34, sufficiently answer the question whether Jeremiah envisages a future of individualised or of socialised religion. The covenant—whether old or new—is what constitutes the *people* of God. Is the interiorisation of faith to be so complete that institutions wither away, and all religious organisation and law and formal ceremony? Jeremiah's particular experience made his assessment of these things rather negative. J. L. McKenzie notes that the major institutions of Israel—tribal confederacy, monarchy, temple, ark—had all foundered by 587; in the fifth century even prophecy dried up. Considering how Israel's institutions had failed her, and even hindered her in her service of God, it is not surprising that in certain passages (and this one above all) Jeremiah gives the impression that the people of God will have no need of organisation and institutions. But if the book as a whole (including 23:4) and the mentality of the time are taken into account, it will be seen that Jeremiah was not 'anti-institutional' in any absolute sense. It was the circumstances of the time that make him, here and there, appear so.

The new covenant and the messiah

Jeremiah's contributions to the messianic theme are in
30, 31, and 23:1–6. In 23, he denounces Israel's disastrous leaders—the shepherds of Yahweh's flock—and
promises in the future a virtuous descendant of David, an
anointed one, messiah, or Christ, who will be a good
king. Beyond Jehoiakim and Zedekiah, Jeremiah dis-
cerns the outline of a righteous mediator of Yahweh's
covenant with his people. Jeremiah goes on to fill in some
of the features of this outline figure. G. von Rad (in *Old
Testament Theology* 2, 218) calls attention to Jer 30:21:

> Their prince shall be one of themselves,
>   their ruler shall come forth from their midst;
> I will make him draw near, and he shall approach me,
>   for who would dare of himself to approach me?
>   says the Lord.

Only one person has this privileged access to Yahweh.
The belief of early Yahwism was that whoever sees God
must die. 'It seems to me', says von Rad, 'to be extremely
characteristic that even in a Messianic prediction Jeremiah is particularly interested in the preconditions of the
saving event as these affect the person involved. In his
view—and here again we recognise Jeremiah—the most
important thing is that the anointed one risks his life, and
in this way holds open access to God in the most personal
terms possible. "Who is it who gives his heart in pledge to
come near to me?" This was one of the hardest questions
that was ever put in ancient Israel. What knowledge of
God and of man was required for it even to be asked!'
(*Old Testament Theology* 2, *219*.)

Beyond Jeremiah: The new covenant in the new testament

The dynamics of the new relationship to God the Father were put into effect by Jesus of Nazareth.

Thierry Maertens writes (in *A Feast in Honour of Yahweh 122*): 'Now it came to pass that one of the faithful, Christ, the faithful one par excellence, celebrated the Passover with a very definite attitude of soul: so definite that it became *the* event in the whole history of salvation: an attitude of submission to his Father, a desire to "serve" his brothers by his expiatory death. So essential is this event that all other rites disappear, become unnecessary, cease to be.'

This seems to explain why the eucharist, though the counterpart to the (annual) passover, was celebrated weekly from the beginning; it subsumed into itself not only the passover, but all the other feasts and gatherings of judaism.

> This is the cup of my blood,
> the blood of the new and everlasting covenant;
> it will be shed for you and
> for all men
> so that sins may be forgiven.
> Do this in memory of me.
>
> (From the Roman canon I)

The new covenant constitutes the new people of God. 'I will be their God, and they shall be my people.' 'They shall all know me'—as Josiah knew God (22:16)—only now, through Christ, in the Spirit, 'I will forgive their iniquity' (31:34)—'this is my blood . . . for the forgiveness of sins' (Mt 26:28)—'so that sins may be forgiven'

(Roman canon I). For a description of the new people of God see 1 Pet 2:9–10.

It is by its celebration in the eucharist that the new covenant constitutes the people of God. 'Do this as a memorial of me' (1 Cor 11:24, 25; Lk 22:19). Karl Rahner writes that these are the central words of the church. 'All other words in the Church are ultimately only preparation, exposition, and defence of these words alone, in which the incarnate Word of God comes into our space and time as our salvation.' (*The Church and the Sacraments* 85–6.)

In what is done, the eucharist, we join ourselves to Christ in the feast of the new covenant; we say to the Father 'you know how firmly . . . we dedicate ourselves to you' (Roman canon I). At the eucharist, the people of God is brought to life, realised, actualised, and manifested in its most intense way of being.

1. How can it be that one of God's covenants (or testaments) is now 'old'? How can anything truly from God need replacing?

2. Does Jeremiah represent a progress in Israel from a 'primitive' collective religious faith to a more personalised one?

3. Does Jeremiah's new covenant prophecy entail any withering away of institutions in the people of God?

4. Why is the collection of writings about Jesus called a 'testament', and 'new'?

5. What about 'old testament' and 'new testament' as christian titles for the two sets of 'scripture'? Can anyone think of better titles?

6. Why should the second covenant be final and everlasting, if the first was not? Why not a third in the future? (The letter to the Hebrews has something on this. See, eg, chapter 8.)

7. What does the new covenant mean in the life of the christian?

8. *How far does Jeremiah picture the new life of man in the future kingdom as an other-worldly life; and how far as a this-worldly life?*

9. *What does Jeremiah's life say to the christian on the subject of success and failure; security and insecurity?*

10. *Jeremiah is often regarded as a hopeless misfit and dreary recluse, withdrawn from the community, and laughably out of touch with real life. Is this a fair description?*

11. *How did Jeremiah know of God's will? Was it*

(a) *by a supernatural speaking of God into his mind, or*

(b) *by the ordinary faith and knowledge of the Jew, joined to close observation and experience of life and affairs, or*

(c) *by both, or*

(d) *in some other way?*

(*Note what he says at 23:18.*)

12. *Can we speak of prophets and prophecy in the church today? What is the etymology of the word 'prophet'? Are the prophets mentioned in 1 Cor 14 like or unlike the prophets of the old testament?*

13. *How far are the theological statements of Jeremiah (as in 31:31) scientific dogmatic propositions, and how far are they persuasive, poetic, exhortatory sayings? In what sense are they true?*

7

Appendix
Jer 46–52;
Lamentations and Baruch

Jer 46–52

The rest of the book of Jeremiah can be classed as appendix. The content is described as 'prophecies against the nations'. Jeremiah is responsible for parts; the rest is only attributed to him.

The 'prophecies' or oracles here are statements declaring God's power over all Judah's neighbours, and God's will for them as put into effect by events. In parts, the genre resembles the sort of psychological warfare put out in the contemporary world by the radio stations of nations at war—statements of huge enemy losses, collapsing morale, columns of refugees, and false ideologies (gods) made to look ridiculous. Yahweh uses Babylon to crush Egypt. Judah's nearer neighbours—Philistia, Moab, Syria—are all laid waste, by no identifiable military power; this is a way of picturing the immediate might of Yahweh. Then Yahweh raises up the Medes to destroy Babylon—and so repay her for the wrong done to Judah. A scroll of prophecies against Babylon is sunk in the Euphrates (51:59) to symbolise the fall of the city, never to rise again.

There, we are told, end 'the words of Jeremiah'. But one more chapter (52) is added. The prose history of the fall of Jerusalem found as 2 Kgs 25 is reproduced as Jer

52 to round off the book of Jeremiah, by showing the fulfilment in history of his prophecies against Judah.

The tragic story is relieved by a ray of hope—it ends with the pardon and release from prison, in 562, in Babylon, of the exiled Jehoiakin, still the legitimate davidic king of Judah, and perhaps the leader of a future restoration (or, if not he, some other son of David?)

Lamentations and Baruch

These two short books are associated with Jeremiah. It is not at all likely that he composed *Lamentations*. But it is easy to see how they came to be attributed to him. They are laments, dirges, poems of mourning and distress, addressed to Jerusalem personified; the city being, after 587, a heap of ruins.

Baruch was not in the Hebrew canon, but was in the Greek Septuagint collection—so it is now in the apocrypha of protestant bibles, but in the canon of catholic bibles. The material relates to the condition of Jewry, exiled and dispersed, but looking towards Jerusalem and the true faith. It is not by Baruch. It probably dates from the second century BC.

The ascription of these two books to Jeremiah and Baruch testifies, however, to the liveliness of their influence and the strength of their authority.

Isaiah 40–66

John Challenor

Introduction

Isaiah 40–66 relates to events which took place in Babylonia shortly before, and in Jerusalem shortly after, 538 BC. In that year, the Judaean exiles in Babylonia were released, to return home to rebuild Jerusalem and their national life.

A note on the names given to the people of God in Is 40–66 will help. The people are sometimes called Israel, or Jacob, after the father of the twelve sons who are regarded as founders of the twelve tribes—the nation. At other times they are called Jerusalem, after their capital city, or Zion, after the hill in the city on which the temple stood. Politically, to their neighbours, they were Judah, Judaeans (hence 'Jews') from the name of the province surrounding Jerusalem.

In 597, and again in 587, and once more in 582, the Babylonians had invaded Judah and taken deliberate steps to render her politically powerless, in order to make the Babylonian empire more secure. They burnt down the temple. They destroyed the walls and buildings of Jerusalem and other towns. They blinded and imprisoned the king. They selected for deportation to Babylonia all the most influential members of society—the administrators, the skilled craftsmen and smiths, the intelligentsia, the soldiers. They left the peasants behind (2 Kgs 24).

167

Jeremiah (52) says 4,600 were marched eastwards, and assuming he means adult males, there may have been 15,000 with women and children. Left behind, in devastated and demoralised Judaea, there may have been at first 100,000 or more, but of these many melted away to Egypt, or lost their identity through intermarriage with neighbouring peoples, or starved. By 538, when the first exiles were able to return, the population of the province of Judaea is estimated at only 20,000.

The exiles in Babylonia were not imprisoned or enslaved. They were *interned*, on land near the city of Babylon, and there left free to support themselves by agriculture and commerce, and to organise their own community life. Exposed as they were to the cultural shock of life among foreigners and to the temptation natural in those days to adopt the worship of the locality, it is important that they were not hindered from meeting together to cultivate their own distinctive faith. They were only six hundred miles away from Jerusalem, and we know from Jeremiah that letters passed between the exiles and home.

But the situation was very serious. After 587, when the temple was destroyed, neither the Judaeans left behind nor those interned in Babylonia were able to carry on the national worship in the familiar surroundings and structures—and one has to remember that for Israel, national consciousness and religious consciousness had been practically the same thing. In the absence of the national temple-shrine and the sacrificial cult on the sacred ground of Mount Zion, Israel had to find new ways of expressing and living her faith—or die, as did the northern tribes who had been deported to Assyria in the eighth century.

The exiles met, as we know from Ezekiel, in private houses and in the open by the banks of canals to hear the word of God read and explained, to address God in prayer, and to transact community business. These gatherings seem to have evolved eventually into the new institution of the synagogue. In addition, the exiles began to make a special point of observing carefully certain features of Israel's law which differentiated them from gentile foreigners—the sabbath rest, circumcision, and avoidance of some foods considered unclean, like pork. Leadership passed from the priestly families to the prophets and teachers and preachers—the scribes and the rabbis of later times. Sociologically, Israel passed abruptly from being the establishment in an independent people to being an exiled minority living abroad under legal restrictions.

In this new situation of the exile, and in the new forms of social organisation to which it gave rise, the author of Is 40–55 taught, trying to give an intelligible explanation of the national disaster of 597 and 587, and trying to communicate a hope for the future without which the survival of Israel's faith in Yahweh would have been in doubt. It is interesting to observe the adaptability displayed by the exiles in finding ways, not merely to preserve the Yahweh faith, but even to broaden its scope and deepen its resources. In spite of Ps 137, they did continue to 'sing the Lord's song in a foreign land'.

Help in dealing with the emergency was available within Israel's own traditions. However great the importance Jerusalem acquired from the time of David, the original Yahwism of Moses was not tied to any fixed sacred place: it was practised in the desert wanderings, and Yahweh was never localised.

Nor was experience of alien worship anything new. Contact with Canaanite religion had been one of Israel's greatest problems ever since her occupation of the

promised land, about 1200. And her national traditions
—the earlier parts of the old testament, already in
existence, supplied ample warning about how to view
foreign cults.

Again, in the century before the exile, in order to
suppress encroaching Canaanite elements from it,
Israel had tried to centralise all her worship under close
supervision in Jerusalem, and so in effect had practically
denuded the rest of Judaea of local worship. This move—
part of the 'deuteronomic reformation'—had introduced
a measure of secularisation into everyday life outside
Jerusalem which may have helped the exiles to adjust to
the much greater degree of secularisation imposed by the
exile.

But along with Israel's readiness to express her faith in
new ways, in a new situation of dispersion on the secular,
even unclean, soil of a foreign land, there went a continuing firm attachment to the Jerusalem temple cult,
and an intense hope of its restoration. Without this hope,
it is difficult to see how the exiles could have resisted the
pressures to become assimilated to their new environment
—wealthy, powerful, sophisticated, and reasonably
tolerant as it was.

Disunity and internal weakness in Babylonia after 550
suggested that Judah's conquerors were in turn going to
be conquered—by the Persian king, Cyrus. Babylon fell
to him in 539 (the story of Belshazzar's feast in Dan 5
gives an impressionistic account of the event). From 539,
for two centuries until the Greek Alexander the Great, a
Persian empire dominated western Asia.

Cyrus pursued a policy of toleration unusual at the
time, positively encouraging former subject peoples to
re-settle their homelands and reconstruct their national
lives and cultures. Cyrus even undertook to pay for the

rebuilding of the Jerusalem temple (Ezra 6:8), though whether the money was ever paid over is doubtful.

From 538, Judaeans dribbled back home, led by those with the more lively faith in Yahweh and the more adventurous pioneer spirit. Many Jews who had settled down physically and mentally in Babylonia, or had become prosperous through commerce, remained behind.

The period from 538 was full of discouragement. The returning exiles found Judaea devastated and depopulated, the roaming-ground of hostile neighbours—Edom, Ammon, Moab, Samaria—and of wild animals. The site of the ruined temple was the scene of a debased, mixed worship. The reconstruction of Israel's national life was slow and difficult. Not till 515, for instance, was the second temple built—a much more modest building than the first. But by sheer persistence the work was done.

Much of Is 40–48 is a defence of the one true God of Israel against the many false and non-existent gods of Babylonia. The religion of Babylonia was a polytheistic system in which Marduk (or Bel) was lord of the gods, having become so by overcoming Tiamat (or Rahab), the monster of watery chaos, and cutting up her body into two parts to make the earth and the sky. Numerous other deities, like the wisdom-god Nebo, were invoked. At the chief religious observance, the annual new year festival in the spring, the king would grasp the right hand of Marduk's statue, and enact the role of Marduk in order to bring under control for the coming year the otherwise uncontrollable forces of nature and political life. The last kings of Babylon—Nabonidus and Belshazzar—omitted the new year festival for some years before 539, much to the indignation of the priests of Marduk and the rest of the Babylonian establishment. They re-instituted it, too late, in 539.

Of the authors of Is 40–66 we know next to nothing, except what we can deduce from the text and by reading between the lines. At least two unknown prophets seem to be responsible. Because their prophecies were copied on the scroll of the eighth-century prophet Isaiah of Jerusalem, these sixth-century prophets are generally known as 2-Isaiah and 3-Isaiah. 2-Isaiah lived in Babylon, and seems to have been the author of 40–55, before 538; 3-Isaiah lived in Jerusalem, and seems to have been the author of 56–66, after 538.

In 40–55, it is possible to isolate two distinct themes. One is the triumphal deliverance of Israel from Babylonia, and divine vengeance on her oppressor. The other is Israel's call to service, to convey God's word to the gentiles. The themes are interwoven, and there is no clear division; all one can say is that in 40–48, the former predominates and in 49–55, the latter. 56–66 are chiefly about the reconstruction of Jerusalem and the discouragements it involved.

The text of Is 40–66 consists of a number of quite distinct sections, separated in the RSV and most other versions by a space. Most scholars think the material originated, not as written compositions, but as addresses spoken by the prophets at occasions of public worship. Later the addresses were written down and edited into the order in which they now stand. It is sometimes uncertain where one section ends and another begins, and it isn't always obvious why the editors put a given section where they did.

These addresses were given just over 2,500 years ago, in a language and in a situation that are totally unfamiliar to us. We take it for granted that a translation is needed. A commentary or extended introduction is also needed. The commentary here, often no more than a summary paraphrase, is supplied in the belief that it is helpful to isolate the keynote on which the rest of a passage depends, and to interpret by re-stating in familiar language. But reading the commentary is a very minor part of the work; the reading of the text, and discussion of it, are far more important.

There is a saying attributed to John Robinson, pastor to the Pilgrim Fathers, about 1620: 'The Lord has more truth yet to break forth out of his holy word.' This is certainly true for every person who studies scripture. But it would be naïve to suggest that the authors of Is 40–66 had us in mind, or our situation, when they spoke. The prophecies yield their application in the church today only when the situation then, the situation now, and what has happened in between, are taken into account.

Book List

For shorter commentary and notes, see the *Jerusalem Bible* (London 1966) and *The Jerome Biblical Commentary* (London 1968). For detailed commentaries, see Claus Westermann *Isaiah 40–66* (London 1969) and C. R. North *The Second Isaiah* (Oxford 1964).

1

The triumph of Yahweh
Is 40–48

Is 40:1–11. In Babylonia, the prophet raises his voice as spokesman for Yahweh, and passes on to his fellow-exiles news of forgiveness and liberation. The motif which dominates all his preaching is stated in 40:2—Israel's warfare, her imprisonment or time of penal servitude, is ended. The disaster Israel incurred through her unfaithfulness was embodied in the historical event of the fall of Judaea and the exile; her forgiveness is being made known in the event of the release and return.

2-Isaiah envisages a joyful march of free men across the Arabian desert back to Jerusalem along a route levelled and smoothed as if for visiting royalty or a liturgical procession—and indeed, it will be both, for Yahweh will be present, revealing himself again through the rehabilitation of his people, as before in Israel's first exodus escape out of Egyptian slavery and across the Sinai desert to the promised land. But the joyful march to freedom is in the future and much encouragement and instruction is needed first. The actual order, 'Depart, go out,' is placed after a long work of preparation, at 52:11.

The liberation is announced by 2-Isaiah as good news —a gospel—of salvation, which the people will proclaim. The Greek translation of the OT (the *Septuagint*) uses for 'good tidings' the word *evangel*, in English 'gospel'.

The voice (40:3, 6) is the closest the prophet takes us to the source of his call. It is the word of the Lord (40:5c). The prophet resists the call (40:6–8) sharing, to a point, the people's despair that the glory of Israel is past—only he believes (40:8b) that though all else may go, king, city, nation, temple, sacrificial ritual, yet God's word stands. God's promises are not broken.

(Note that the voice in 40:3 is transposed in the Septuagint into a 'voice crying in the wilderness', and comes in the NT to be applied to John the Baptist: an illustration of the freedom with which scripture was handled in its formative period.)

Is 40:12–31. To what 2-Isaiah says in this section, one clue is 40:27: the exiles naturally feel rejected, abandoned, and sorry for themselves, and express their feelings in a lament in psalm style. A second clue is 40:19: no doubt the exiles felt the temptation to transfer their loyalty, or part of it, to the local gods of victorious Babylon, who on the face of it were more powerful than Yahweh. To counter these movements of faithlessness, the prophet extols Yahweh as supreme over nations (12–17), over princes (18–24), and over the heavenly bodies worshipped as deities in Babylon (25–26). And he extols Yahweh, not in the familiar way to date as Israel's God, but in a new way as the one and only God of the whole world. 2-Isaiah must count as one of the most influential men of all time. He pioneered an idea of God held without question till very recent times in the classical theology of judaism, Islam, and christianity.

1. What sort of evidence does the prophet point to in his effort to revive faltering faith and hope?

2. In the light of what has emerged so far, consider the diffi-

culties of faith in an unfriendly environment—and in a friendly
one.

Is 41:1–7. The debate is on. Yahweh calls the people to
argue it out with him publicly like a case in civil law. He
challenges them to refute his argument that it is he who
has called the conqueror from the east (and from the
north—41:25—the Hebrew way of saying north-east).
In 550–547 Cyrus, king of Persia, was winning sensational
victories, and the day could be foreseen when Babylon
would fall to him. The word for victory in 41:2 is in
Hebrew *tsedeq*, not merely military victory, but the
establishment of justice, prosperity, and righteousness—
the new order of things willed by God. Yahweh is Lord
and controller of history, and (41:5–7) well may the
gentiles in alarm set to work trying to manufacture
stronger idols—dead loss as idols are (41:28–29).

Is 41:8–16. Yahweh has not cast off his chosen people
Israel. On the contrary, he is her redeemer, her *go'el*—
the Hebrew term denoting that member of the family
responsible for coming to the help of any other member
who may be in trouble, from debt or enslavement or
false accusations, and so on. Yahweh holds Israel by her
right hand, and will vindicate her; she will not be
crushed—she will crush.

Is 41:17–20. Yahweh will transform the desert into a
fertile oasis. Here is a picture of the action of God which
by allusion brings together the remoter past (the paradise garden), the near past (the exodus from Egypt), the
near future (the return home from exile after 538) and
the distant future (the consummation at the end).

Is 41:21–29. Idols can say and do nothing about the

future; Yahweh alone reveals and controls the course of history, and he has given news of it to Israel.

Bishop Larrain, of Talca, Chile, said at the second Vatican Council, 'we must listen not only to teachers, but also to events.' Does the church overdo the teachers at the expense of the events? On which does 2-Isaiah base his message? Is it possible to separate teachers and events?

Is 42:1–9. The prophet is exploring relationships between Israel, Yahweh, and the rest of the world. (This is one way of describing Is 40–55 as a whole.)

He now pictures a 'servant' to whom God gives the mission of bringing forth justice to the world. This justice is in Hebrew *mishpat*—judgement, law, right, connoting the whole will and purpose of Yahweh. And the nations are the gentiles, all mankind apart from Israel. The servant's demeanour is described negatively (42:2–4) as if in contrast with another servant, possibly Cyrus, or some prophet like Amos given to denunciation. Now, perhaps, self-effacement will be the way to gain a hearing, to make God known in the world (42:6), and to effect liberation (42:7).

So far the nature of the servant's mission is clearer to us than the identity of the servant. Look at the picture and try to bring the figure of the servant into focus. Is it Israel, personified? Or, since the servant is a covenant to Israel (42:6), is it a faithful minority within Israel? There are three more 'servant-songs' or poems, in chapters 49, 50 and 52–53, which may help to clarify the mystery. But we must not assume the mystery is soluble, when we find the prophet being deliberately cryptic and enigmatic.

The former things (42:9) are probably the events connected with the fall of Jerusalem in 587, as prophe-

sied by Jeremiah and others. The new things are plainly
the imminent release and return of Israel.

Is 42:10–17. At this good news, the prophet raises his
baton and calls for a psalm in praise of Yahweh, who
admits he has given the appearance of inactivity while
his people have been in exile, but who now promises
decisive, even violent, action, as at the exodus from
Egypt. The blind are the disheartened exiles who cannot
read the signs of impending liberation.

Is 42:18–25. The prophet reminds Israel that her exile
has been due, not to the military and political power of
Babylonia, but to God's will that Israel should suffer
temporarily in order to realise her sin and faithlessness.
Faced with the fact of the exile—Israel's first experience
of a 'separation of church and state'—the prophet
develops a new argument for faith in Yahweh. The old
argument that Yahweh brought his people military
victory and security and prosperity was no longer usable.
2-Isaiah's new argument is that whatever word Yahweh
speaks, whether it is of victory or of defeat, is carried into
effect by events.

*What assurance have we that the prophet is right in seeing the
hand of God in events like the fall of Jerusalem and the release of
the exiles by Cyrus, which others explain without reference to God?*

Is 43:1–7. Yahweh loves Israel as a father loves his
family. All the dispersed and exiled Israelites—in Egypt,
to the south and west, in what used to be Assyria, to the
north, as well as in Babylonia to the east—all will be
gathered in and reunited as Yahweh's people.

Is 43:8–13. In court, witnesses are called in the case of
Yahweh versus the idols. For Yahweh, Israel is called,

disheartened as she is, and into her mouth the evidence is put: the events of the time reveal that Yahweh is the only God and saviour.

Is 43:14–21. The defeat of Babylonia (also called Chaldaea) means a new exodus for Israel. In the key verses, 18–19, the prophet astonishingly tells his audience to forget the former things (the original exodus event and the traditions of the past) and to look at the new thing Yahweh is doing—the liberation soon to take place. Taken literally, this must have sounded blasphemous in traditionalist Israelite ears. Possibly the prophet is asserting, with some rhetorical overstatement, the magnitude of the coming act of deliverance. Possibly he is using the term 'remember' in a technical liturgical sense and suggesting that, in the future, Israel's reconstructed worship will be a commemoration, not of the exodus or any secondary theme like the founding of the monarchy, but of the return from the exile, a new beginning. Or the prophet's message may have been 'stop living in the past, and look towards the future!' And it might not have been heard unless it contained some element calculated to shock.

Further, the prophet is speaking eschatologically, about the end of the world and the consummation of history as brought forward into the here and now by God's action. In so far as the 'age to come' is made present and a new order established, all that is past is radically superseded. This may explain 43:18. Von Rad says (*Old Testament Theology*, II, p 118): 'The prophetic teaching is only eschatological when the prophets expelled Israel from the safety of the old saving actions and suddenly shifted the basis of salvation to a future action of God.'

Is 43:22–28. Again in the context of a lawsuit, Yahweh goes over old ground with Israel, ascribing her exile to her disobedience from the very beginning—from the time of her first father, the founder of the nation, Jacob. About worship, Yahweh seems to say that even his modest requirements were not met; instead, he received from his people nothing but sin.

Do the people of God today preoccupy themselves unduly with 'former things', the past, at the expense of 'a new thing', the present and future?

Is 44:1–5. The new Israel will be given the gifts of God's Spirit to make her a charismatic community. 44:5 seems to mean that gentiles will join Israel.

Is 44:6–23. Between two short passages extolling the one true God, comes the first of the few prose passages of Is 40–66. This is a satire on idol-worship, a careful mock-serious description of the manufacturing process, calculated to convey the ludicrous solemn stupidity of the idol-worshipper. This is Israel's defence of her own characteristic belief and worship, expressed negatively in the form of a protest against polytheism and 'graven images', whether Canaanite or Babylonian. Israel found it revolting that any phenomenon or power within nature—agricultural fertility, or sex, or water, or heavenly body, or any other supposed manipulator of earth or human life—should be personified, divinised, represented in images, and worshipped. If an image of God must be spoken of, is not man himself—at a distance—the image and likeness of God? It is helpful to remember that Gen 1:1–2:4, and the rest of the 'Priestly' material of the Pentateuch, was probably being worked on actively during the exile in Babylonia, at the same time as 2-Isaiah was teaching.

Von Rad states: 'This awareness of the barrier which men erect between themselves and God by means of images is . . . Israel's greatest achievement.' The idol, the fetish—anything in nature endowed falsely with a value it doesn't have—threatens to enslave, to debase, and to isolate human beings, and to reduce human community to meaninglessness and incoherence. How strongly Israel felt about idolatry is evident in Wisdom 14:27: 'for the worship of idols not to be named (ie non-existent) is the beginning and cause and end of every evil.'

Is 44:24–28. The prophet at last announces, for the first time, clearly and by name, that it is Cyrus whom Yahweh has chosen as his regent to bring about the restoration of Israel.

1. What relevance has Israel's rejection of idols for us today?

2. Can the scientific, empirical, secularising attitude of much of the contemporary world—the pragmatic approach to nature and reality as something at man's disposal—be traced back to any extent to 2-Isaiah and the Babylonian exile? Has man used nature irresponsibly—abused and defiled it?

Is 45:1–8. A surprise: Yahweh gives the title 'messiah' to the gentile king, Cyrus. But it was only later that 'messiah', 'the Lord's anointed', acquired a specialised meaning and was restricted to Christ. King Saul had been the Lord's anointed, and in the sixth century the title could still be used of any Israelite king by reason of the ritual at his enthronement. That the title is given to Cyrus is a sign that the prophet recognises Yahweh's universal sovereignty. It was not a permanent charism for Cyrus; he was used as Yahweh's agent just for this occasion.

The commissioning of Cyrus is described in the language of the royal enthronement liturgy of Babylon. The wording of 45: 1–2 has parallels in the inscription on the Cyrus cylinder—a clay cylinder of about 538 describing the capture of Babylon. On it, we read that Marduk 'scoured all the lands for a friend, seeking for the upright prince . . . to take his hand. He called Cyrus . . . he made him take the road to Babylon, and he went at his side like a friend and comrade.' (This is not to say that 2-Isaiah knew anything of the Cyrus cylinder; he was presumably teaching before 538. The parallels are probably due to 2-Isaiah and the Cyrus cylinder making common use of the conventional language of the annual enthronement liturgy.) 45: 8 is a short hymn addressed to Yahweh, concluding the important statement about Cyrus.

The Cyrus prophecy (44:24–45:8) focuses the whole message of 2-Isaiah on a coming historical event, makes a heathen king instrumental in Israel's salvation, and declares that God's purpose in all this is to make himself, the creator of all, known to all mankind. The consequences seem to be momentous. First, in conferring a saving role on an outsider, Yahweh declares that his kingdom is separate from and independent of any particular political community, even of Israel. If God's grace, even at the level of public events shaping the course of world history, is given outside the people of God, to worshippers of other (false) gods, where does it leave the traditional institutions? All the familiar categories of thought seem to be upset, and all securities threatened.

Secondly, Yahweh is (45:7) the creator of darkness

and woe—of evil! The story of creation in Gen 1 carefully avoided calling God creator of the original chaos
and darkness. The story of the fall of man in Gen 3 carefully ascribed evil in creation not to God but to the
perversity of a creature. This very subtle form of dualism,
like the manicheism and gnosticism and more thorough-
going dualism of the ancient near east, had the effect of
exonerating God, to some degree, from responsibility for
the evil of the world. Now 2-Isaiah in telling us that
Yahweh is creator of all that is, without exception, does
not hesitate to draw the full implications, and state them
explicitly. The wonder of it all—as well as the acute
difficulty—is expressed in 45:15: 'truly, thou art a God
who hidest thyself.'

Is 45:9–13. The prophet answers the predictable objection of the traditionalist Israelite that Yahweh would not
call a gentile to any saving role in Israel's history.

Is 45:14–25. The gentiles will come and join Israel in
worshipping Yahweh. ('In chains': as defeated by
Cyrus as subjugated by Israel? Or this may be an interpolation which has strayed in from 60:14.)

The calling in of the gentiles has been spoken of before
by 2-Isaiah, in 42:6 and 44:5. And the theme is not
confined to 2-Isaiah: the call of Abraham is presented as
an event which will bring a blessing on all mankind.
Once God's special choice of Israel existed in Israel's
theology side by side with unqualified monotheism, then
it became logically inevitable, for consistency, that a new
belief must emerge. It had to be either a new belief in
Israel's election, not as a restricted privilege, but for the
service of all mankind. Or it had to be a new belief in the
total iniquity of the gentiles and their total rejection
from God's sight as if they had never existed.

In the world of the sixth century BC, when faith and worship were otherwise coterminous with nation and race, these steps towards universalism were a striking innovation. Lindblom says 'the conversion of the pagan nations is conceived of as a divine wonder of an eschatological nature, and Israel is involved as an instrument in Yahweh's hand, by witnessing and suffering' (*Prophecy in Ancient Israel*, p 428).

There is room for some difference of opinion on how complete 2-Isaiah's universalism was. In his picture of Israel and the gentiles as no longer enemies but joining together to worship God, there are some elements suggesting the subordination, even the subjection, of the gentiles. John Bright's explanation is this: 'A broad fresh current poured into the main stream of Israel's faith; although one might say it mingled poorly, it could never be sealed off' (*History of Israel*, p 339).

It mingled poorly. So strong was the nationalist consciousness of Israel that it would have been astonishing if a fully universalist point of view had suddenly found full and undisputed expression. (The theme of the call of the gentiles recurs at 49:6–7, 52:13–53:12 and 63:1–6.)

1. Is 2-Isaiah's teaching so far truly universalistic, or is it a sort of Israelite imperialism?

2. How far does the church, even now, manifest in visible practice its universalistic (international, supra-racial) character?

3. Does God make himself known through the history of Israel and the church, or through the life of the whole world?

Is 46:1–7. Bel was Marduk, lord of the Babylonian gods, under another name. Nebo, or Nabu, was the god of wisdom, whose name kings like Nebuchadnezzar and Nabonidus compounded with their own. Note the excited staccato rhythm with which 46 begins. The images of the

7—P. I

foreign gods are carted off, helpless, among the refugees! Of 46:1–4 Westermann says: 'This passage constitutes the bible's most profound utterance on the representation of a god by an image. Here, the second commandment has borne its richest harvest. For 2-Isaiah, the difference between Yahweh, and the gods who can be represented by images . . . lies in the realm of history.' When disaster strikes, the images are carried by men and beasts; the God of Israel, in contrast, carries his people.

Looking ahead to the fall of Babylon before it happened, 2-Isaiah is proved wrong about some of the details of the picture. The Persian conqueror did not in fact exile the Babylonian gods—he retained and venerated them. This inaccuracy of detail tells us something of the nature of prophecy—and also perhaps of the unexpectedness of Cyrus' behaviour.

Is 46:8–11. 'Remember the former things of old' exactly contradicts, on the surface, 43:18. It may be that 43:18 is a rather untypical formulation, and that 46:9 is the standard teaching. The claims of past history and tradition cannot be ignored altogether, however radical or revolutionary the change. On the other hand, the prophet may, in 46:9, be appealing not to tradition in general but to those particular displays (like the exodus) of God's mighty power in it, as precedents for new belief and hope in the coming new act of salvation.

Is 46:12–13. The words 'deliverance' and 'salvation' occur here twice. They belong to a cluster of words used by 2-Isaiah which include justice, peace, truth, righteousness, and victory.

This 'deliverance' (*tsedaqah*) is the divine gift of a new order which 2-Isaiah says over and over again is coming. It is the state of things in which all man's relationships—

with God, other men, the world—are healed and set right; and hence in which man is righteous and holy, faithful to the covenant, and freed from all the false and defective relationships which form the state of sin and guilt.

1. The calling of Cyrus, a Persian, is attributed by 2-Isaiah to Israel's God, and by the Cyrus cylinder to Babylon's god. Does this, and Cyrus's adoption of Babylonian gods, suggest that a general syncretism was going on—an exchange of gods—a disguised indifference?

2. Is it possible for faith in past tradition (the former things of old) to militate against true faith in God—to be even a sort of idolatry?

3. How separate from 'this world' is the 'world to come' in which 2-Isaiah locates salvation?

Is 47. This chapter takes up the theme of 46:1–2—the fall of Babylon. It proclaims at length in advance the coming fall of the whole empire, all its power and privilege, its intellectual achievements and religious observances.

Some put it in the category of the 'taunt-song'—though there is no mockery or jeering in it. It is a serious theological statement of the complete and tragic failure of an erroneous ideology. Oracles against foreign nations, enemies of Israel, are familiar in the OT; they are negative statements of Israel's salvation. Here the prophet gives an explanation for the humiliation of Babylonia (47:6–8) —Yahweh used Babylon to punish Israel, but Babylon behaved mercilessly and arrogantly and so itself deserved destruction. The chapter ends with a denunciation of Babylonian astrological worship and sorcery.

In the time of 2-Isaiah, political power was commonly

equated with the possession of soldiers, arms and resources ('coming out of the barrel of a gun'). 2-Isaiah was sophisticated enough to know the importance, too, of a coherent ideology uniting the people and doing justice to the known facts of experience. From this point of view, Babylon had already fallen before Cyrus arrived at the gates.

Does this chapter seem to display an anti-Babylonian nationalism discordant with 2-Isaiah's universalist theme?

Is 48:1–11. Two themes mingle, a dark one and a light one. The dark one is Yahweh's blame for Israel, as obstinate and unresponsive. The light one is his promise that Israel will hear new things. The dark theme may be the record of an address by the prophet on a day of fasting and repentance. Some, though, argue it was written in later by another prophetic writer, on the grounds that 2-Isaiah, though he blames Israel for her conduct before the exile, regarded his own time and the future as times of forgiveness and salvation.

The light theme repeats the striking 43:18; 'new things'. The former things and the new things have this in common, that all are from Yahweh. The former things (from Abraham to the fall of Jerusalem in 587) were prophesied and they happened. The new things (liberation and return after 538) are being prophesied, and they will happen.

But there is also a great difference: the two periods are separated by the fifty-year interval of the exile. The prophet exerts himself to persuade Israel to lift her eyes from the past and look toward the future. The prophet is leading up to a call for action and movement (48:20).

Is 48:12–22. The scene suggested by 48:14 is a sabbath

assembly for worship. Peace (48:18)—*shalom*—is parallel
with righteousness—a comprehensive right ordering of all
relationships, which the wicked (48:22) conspicuously
lack.

*Through what he says in 47 and 48 of Israel and Babylon,
does 2-Isaiah tell us today anything about the church and her less
obvious but no less real captors and oppressors—as some maintain,
the 'first world' of wealthy white western culture, and the 'second
world' of established communism? (The church was said to be in
'Babylonian captivity' by Petrarch in the fourteenth century when
the popes were under French political influence, and by Luther in
the sixteenth when, he believed, wrong views of the eucharist
prevailed.)*

2

Israel's suffering and service
Is 49–55

With the next chapter (Is 49) we seem to be in a rather
different world; time has moved on. The previous nine
chapters dealt with the coming triumph of Yahweh and
Israel, through Cyrus, over Babylon and idolatry.
Chapters 49–55, which speak of Israel often as 'Zion' or
'Jerusalem', centre around the rehabilitation of the
people and their city, and the suffering and service
through which it will be achieved.

Is 49:1–7. In the second 'servant song', the servant tells
the world how Yahweh chose him, how he grew despon-
dent (49:4), and how the Lord enlarged his commission,
from rebuilding Israel to imparting knowledge of God to
the whole gentile world.

Is it clear yet who the servant is? The prophet? Israel
as a whole? Superficially, 49:3 calls the servant Israel.
But 49:6 says the servant has a mission to Israel. So
'Israel' in 49:3 could be an interpolation, by some well-
meaning copyist trying to help the puzzled reader.

At a deeper level, some of the text (for example, 'called
from the womb of my mother') suggests an individual.
A case could be made for saying the servant is the
prophet, who first had a mission to bring back Israel to
God; who felt he had failed; who yet had really succeeded;

191

and who was therefore given a wider mission to the gentile world.

The prophet himself, however, may not have known who the servant was. He may have been communicating a vision that was less than clear to himself. He may have been pioneering across the frontiers of accepted thought and conventional language, and inviting Israel, or any Israelite who would, to glimpse a possibility that was new and terrifying.

In 49:7, God is 'redeemer', a term already mentioned at 41:14. In our time, 'next-of-kin' approximately renders *go'el*, 'redeemer', except that allowance has to be made for the relative decline of the family as an institution. Rulers will look with admiration at Israel, whom they once despised, amazed by the steadfast faithfulness of Yahweh her God.

Is 49:8–13. The theme of liberated Israel repeated.

Is 49:14–21. When the people repeat their despairing lament, Yahweh answers with loving words to Zion as his wife, who was formerly bereaved, barren, exiled, put away, but is now restored and the mother of many children.

Is 49:22–26. And though Judah is too small for the new population (49:20), even more of her dispersed people are repatriated with rejoicing.

2-Isaiah used the familiar term go'el *(family redeemer, advocate, protector) as a symbol or metaphor for God. What symbols help us most to think and speak of God now?*

Is 50:1–3. Yahweh defends himself, as if in a court case again, against Israel's reproaches. He never divorced her. There was nothing more than a separation, due to her unfaithfulness. There can be forgiveness and reconciliation. And Yahweh has power, not only to forgive, but also to restore Israel—think again of what he did at the exodus. No one appears for Israel, to pursue the case against Yahweh.

Is 50:4–9. The third servant song presents the servant as a faithful disciple who patiently endures the persecution provoked by his ministry of sustaining the weary. Those who think the servant is an individual argue that we have here innocent suffering, so that the servant cannot be Israel, whose sufferings, the prophet insists, were deserved.

The way the persecution and ill-treatment are portrayed (50:6) suggests two possible models: the actual sufferings of the prophet Jeremiah, and the ritual ill-treatment of some eastern kings at enthronement festivals when they took on themselves the sins of their people.

Is 50:10–11. A call to Jews and gentiles to follow the servant in faith, rather than walk in darkness or follow the misleading light of their own fire.

Does the third servant song show signs of being part of 2-Isaiah's autobiography?

Is 51:1–8. A whole constellation of Israelite 'hurrah-words' shine here, denoting the kingdom of God which is coming with the release and return—deliverance, law, justice, salvation, righteousness, and the rule of God.

51:1–2 appeals to past tradition—the 'former things'—as evidence to convince Israel about the 'new thing'. In particular, 'blessings for all the families of the earth' were promised to Abraham (51:2), and are now coming (51:4–5).

Is 51:9–11. As if he felt he had at last convinced the people of the truth of his message, and that they were now ready, the prophet turns and urges Yahweh to act. He invokes Yahweh boldly in the unmistakable language of the Babylonian cult, as the one who having slain the original sea-monster of chaos (Rahab, or Tiamat), proceeded to the creation of dry land and life. This is astonishing when you consider Israel's usual fierce zeal to keep Yahweh clearly distinct from the myths and deities of pagan worship. But second thoughts help you to realise that even Israel's formal creation story in Gen 1 borrows some Babylonian creation motifs, and that the OT does not have a single clearly worked-out theology of the beginning—or of the end.

Parallel with the deliverance that was creation followed the exodus deliverance. Both were a creation, and both a deliverance. Both were a drawing of dry land and new life from watery nothingness and chaos. And soon will come a third parallel, the return of Zion after 538 and the reclamation of the desolate wastes of Jerusalem and Judaea.

The prophet links creation and redemption closely together. Later, christian scholastic theology, or the popular teaching based on it, separated them, envisaging first the creation of the world and nature, and then secondly the redeeming intervention of God to rescue fallen man. 2-Isaiah does not make this distinction, but sees God's design and activity—and hence, man and nature—as one. (St Paul, in Col 1:15–20, for example, also links creation and redemption together—in Christ. When we know the end of a story, we understand better the events at the beginning.)

Is 51:12–23. Further assurances of salvation, in terms now familiar. Israel's sufferings will be lifted from her and placed on her oppressors.

In Is 51:9 and Gen 1:2, creation seems to be part of the historical process—it seems to be an ordering of something that was already there. This does not quite coincide with the doctrine of creation from nothing. Is one view mixed up with mythology and the other in some way 'scientifically true'?

Is 52:1–2. The rehabilitation of Israel is spoken of in terms of 'cleanness' or ritual purity, acquired through keeping certain rules. During the exile, Israel nourished her self-identity over against the gentiles by the distinctive observances of sabbath-keeping, male circumcision, and food regulations (no pork, for example).

Is 52:3–6. This is an obscure passage. It seems to say that Yahweh's acts are free, gratuitous, independent of man. But the exile was not gratuitous; it was deserved. So what becomes of Yahweh's original free choice of Israel, and the gratuitousness of the gift of liberation now? The matter recurs in chapters 54 and 59 in the form of the question of salvation by works or by faith, by law or by grace. One point is clear: Israel is to know by her release that Yahweh is at work.

Is 52:7–10. Of the bringer of good tidings (the 'evangelist') Gerhard Friedrich writes: 'He is the herald who precedes the people on their return from Babylon to Zion. All Jerusalem stands on the towers and walls expecting the column of returning exiles. Then they see the messenger on the top of the hill. "Peace and salvation, Yahweh is king", he cries to them. He proclaims the victory of Yahweh over the whole world. . . . The messenger publishes it, and the new age begins. . . . By the fact that he declares the restoration of Israel, the new creation of the world, the inauguration of the eschatological age, he brings them to pass' (Kittel, *Theological Dictionary*).

This central proclamation—'your God reigns'—occurs in the liturgy, in the enthronement psalms (eg 47, 93, 96–99), and this suggests that some of the picture in 52:7–10 is drawn from the experience of worship in Jerusalem before the exile. (Unless, as a few argue, the enthronement psalms are post-exilic, and borrow the language of 2-Isaiah.) 'Your God reigns': with the collapse of Israel's monarchy, the expectation of God's kingdom had been pushed forward into the distant future end-time. Now in Is 52 it becomes a hope for the immediate near future. Eschatology had become actuality.

Is 52:11–12. The prophet gives the order for the exiles to return, in a new exodus, though this time not as fugitives. 2-Isaiah nowhere gives any historical account of the actual return. In 7–10, he gives a theological account, non-historical in so far as the towers and walls are already rebuilt. In 11–12 he gives the word for the return. But in so far as the great event is delineated, it is not the return, *historically*, but the presence of God and his rule, *liturgically*.

What is the connection between the events of revelation and salvation, on the one hand, and public worship, on the other?

Is 52:13–53:12. In the fourth and last of the servant songs, Yahweh speaks at the beginning and the end. In 53:1–10 the uncertainty remains—is it the prophet, or Israel, or even the gentiles, who speak?

To paraphrase and summarise: Yahweh proclaims the triumphal enthronement of his humiliated servant in the sight of the horrified gentiles. The servant was sick, and rejected. He bore, and lifted from them, the sin of the many. He was executed ignominiously, and buried in the criminals' grave in wicked wealthy Babylon. He lives again to see the fruit of his suffering—the many made righteous.

If the servant is basically Israel, we have an intelligible interpretation: God's people serve him by suffering with hope, and by this striking paradox they are instrumental in bringing new life to themselves and knowledge of God to the rest of the world. In the context of the prophet's whole message, he seems to intend the figure of the servant to be a summons to every Israelite—and every gentile and later believer—who is willing to respond, to accept suffering freely as the way to life and the kingdom. If this is so, then ask not who the servant is—you yourself, reader, are the servant. In this interpretation, the question whether the servant is an individual or a group becomes irrelevant; one may as well ask is the prodigal son (Lk 15) an individual or a group?

Within this broad general understanding of the servant, there is room for many possibilities. Von Rad argues that in constructing the servant-figure, 2-Isaiah uses features of the life of Moses, the prototype of the prophets. If the return is a second exodus, it needs a second Moses to lead it. Others say the servant is 2-Isaiah himself. One suggestion is that 2-Isaiah, in the exile, led an anti-Babylonian underground movement and was executed; that he wrote the first three servant songs; and that the fourth song is by a disciple (3-Isaiah?) who saw his death and arrived at a new understanding of it. (The idea of death and resurrection was not unfamiliar in the ancient near east: the rites of the Tammuz cult celebrated the dying and rising of a vegetation and fertility god. And the scapegoat of Lev 16 was a familiar symbol in Israel.)

1. Read Acts 8:26–38. Does this help us to identify the servant?

2. Read Lk 4:16–30. Did Christ interpret his mission on the model of the servant?

3. Read Acts 13:47, Gal 1:15 and Rom 15:21. Paul presents his mission in terms of the Isaianic servant. What do you make of this?

Is 54:1–10. Zion will be repopulated. Yahweh speaks to Israel as a man to his wife, promising a new family and everlasting faithfulness. (Childlessness was a grave misfortune in Israel: fertility was highly prized.)

Is 54:11–17. 54:11 indicates that this oracle was spoken while the exiles were still in Babylon. Zion will be a place of beauty, righteousness, and security. The key to the chapter seems to be 54:17: 'this is the heritage of the servants of the Lord.' The fruit of the suffering of the servant (53) is described here (54) as it affects Israel—rehabilitates her as Yahweh's beloved bride.

To all the various eschatological blessings promised to Israel— a rebuilt city, a repopulated land, etc—what are the corresponding blessings for the church?

Is 55:1–5. An open invitation to all, Jew and gentile, to come and enjoy the blessings of the covenant. This is the only occasion on which 2-Isaiah alludes to David. He seems to have no time for the idea (very prominent in 1-Isaiah) of a future davidic kingship. For 2-Isaiah, the blessings promised to David are transferred to Israel as a people (3–5).

Is 55:6–13. Bound up with the physical return to Jerusalem is the moral return to Yahweh (55:7)—to right living, instead of sin, reached by repentance, conversion, *metanoia*.

'My thoughts are not your thoughts'. Some take this as repeating the theme of God's unlimited power (40:12–31). Others think it means God is near and ready with forgiveness in a way that Israel, left to herself, finds it hard to credit.

2-Isaiah concludes with a climax of exodus imagery.

1. Considering the context as well as the words, do 55 : 8–9 seem to mean that God is far and remote, or near and present (or both) ?

2. Can you explain why 2-Isaiah reinterprets the promises to king David as promises to the people generally? Has this interpretation any implications for us today?

Introduction to Is 56–66

The scene is now Jerusalem, after the return there of the first few exiles in 537. Most biblical scholars think these chapters are the work of a follower of 2-Isaiah, another equally anonymous prophet generally known as 3-Isaiah. (He does speak in the first person in 61:1 and 62:1.) In contrast with the prolific hopes of 40–55, these later chapters betray some disappointment at the slow pace and meagre results of the restoration that actually took place.

3-Isaiah lays great stress on the observance of the sabbath rest. This, with other legal requirements such as male circumcision and abstinence from foods like pork considered unclean, helped Israel in exile to survive as a distinct and identifiable community. Historians speak of the beginning at this point of a new phase in Israel's life —the phase of 'judaism', which has lasted into the present day, in which the ritual temple worship and priesthood recede into the background (even, in the first century AD, ceasing to exist); and in which there come into the foreground verbal prayer, study of scripture, instruction, and detailed rules of life based on the law of Moses.

3-Isaiah was active some time after 537 and before 520. Is 60:13 shows the second temple not yet built, and we know from other sources (Haggai, Ezra and Persian history) that the rebuilding took place in 520–516.

It is generally thought that chapters 60–62 are the nucleus of 3-Isaiah's message, and that certain sections in 56–59 and 63–66 are by others associated with him. The content of 56–66 shows that 3-Isaiah was a disciple of 2-Isaiah, concerned to continue and apply his message in different conditions not envisaged by the earlier prophet.

3
After the return
Is 56–66

Is 56:1–2. Active in Babylon before the release, 2-Isaiah had envisaged justice and righteousness and the rule of God in general terms, as shortly to arrive. 3-Isaiah, faced in Jerusalem with the actual intractable everyday problems of the national reconstruction, approaches the same justice and righteousness by way of practical programme of obedience to the regulations of the law—the sabbath, for example.

Is 56:3–8. 3-Isaiah deals with some of the practical issues raised by 2-Isaiah's theoretical universalism. Gentiles and even eunuchs, formerly disqualified from full membership of the worshipping community, are now to be accepted into it. The eunuch will gain God's approval by keeping the covenant rules. Gentiles who join the community can even minister in the temple (when it is built), because it is a house of prayer for all peoples (56:7). (Note again the way the gospels—Mk 11:17; Mt 21:13; Lk 19:46—quote the words 'my house shall be called a house of prayer', not with the original contrast between Israel and all peoples, but with a new contrast between prayer and profanity. Mt and Lk even omit 'for all peoples'. This indicates the flexibility, already noted in Is 40:3 and Mt 3:3, with which scripture is used within scripture, even by Christ himself.)

This very significant passage (3–8) marks a change in the basis of membership of the people of God, and therefore in its character. Up to the exile, membership was based almost entirely on birth into the Israelite nation. Now, with the return, membership will be based more and more on the free choice of persons deciding to commit themselves to Yahweh. From being a closed community, the people of God becomes open. It takes a step away from being a national 'establishment' body, in the direction of what later times called a 'gathered' church. (The word 'gathered' is used in 56:8.)

Is 56:9–12. This is in the style of the pre-exilic prophets, and may be an old familiar protest brought back into play. The ruling class pursue their selfish interests, dislike the prospect of change, and do all they can to maintain the status quo, while the people suffer.

Was there not a danger that by implementing 2-Isaiah's programme and admitting gentiles, the community would lose its identity and destroy itself? Examine the conflicting claims, then and now, of universalism and sectarianism.

Is 57:1–13. The prophet attacks the idolatrous observances—sorcery, child-sacrifice, libations, domestic idols, and Baal-worship (apostasy, spoken of as adultery)—which had regularly seduced Israel over the centuries, and which probably flourished exceptionally in Judah among those left behind during the exile, when there was less to counteract them. Yahweh will expose this spurious 'righteousness' (57:12).

Is 57:14–21. The message of 2-Isaiah in 40:3 was a literal one: 'prepare the way of the Lord ... make straight in the desert a highway for our God.' 3-Isaiah now re-applies the message figuratively in the sense of a new way of life, a reformation of conduct, a transfer from the ranks of the wicked to the ranks of the righteous, for whom there is peace. For Yahweh who inhabits eternity lives too with the humble and contrite man.

Why does the church now not take a hostile view, like Israel generally, of other religions?

Is 58:1–12. The prophet speaks to the people on a day of fasting—there were some days of lamentation every year, since the fall of the first temple in 587. Admitting that there is good will (58:2), he makes the point, familiar since Amos, that fasting which accompanies and punctuates oppression and exploitation of the workers and the poor is no fasting as far as Yahweh is concerned. Only if this discrepancy is remedied, and if contempt and slander are avoided (58:9), will the community be on the way to reconstruction. 58:12 is a topical reference to the current physical rebuilding programme of the city.

Is 58:13–14. To the argument on fasting is added a parallel argument on keeping the sabbath.

From a group of christians in the Tiradentes prison at São Paulo in Brazil, there came at Easter 1970 a paper headed 'Easter message to our brothers in Brazil,' and signed 'The Church in prison'. It quoted Is 40–66 many times, especially chapter 58, saying 'we are experiencing in our bodies Isaiah's vision of the suffering servant . . . when will we become the new man, freed from this decadent society? . . . The joy of remaining faithful more than compensates for tortures'. Is this a right way to understand and use the prophecies?

Is 59:1–8. The background of this chapter seems to be

the intense discouragement in Jerusalem after some years of trying to rebuild the city physically and the community morally. So the prophet gives the standard explanation: things are bad, not because of any weakness or remoteness on the part of Yahweh, but because the people's misdeeds have separated them from him.

Is 59:9–15. The people seem to accept this, and break into a lament or penitential psalm.

Is 59:15–21. There is nothing that man can do, but Yahweh himself will intervene like a man of war, faithful to his covenant. (Of Yahweh's violent intervention, there is a more detailed picture in chapter 63.)

There seems to be an inconsistency in scripture. At one time we are told that God loves and rewards men when and because they are good. At other times we are told he loves men anyway, because he is good. One is the way of works and law; the other is the way of faith and grace. How does 3-Isaiah fit with 2-Isaiah on this point? (See chapter 54.)

Is 60:1–18. The chapter pursues the theme of Yahweh's intervention. Some joyful liturgical occasion seems to have been the setting, or at least provided the prophet with his theme and imagery—the glory of the new Jerusalem. To the light of the Lord's glory in Jerusalem will flock Jews of the dispersion and gentiles from far places (rather obsequiously) bringing rich offerings to give God praise in the (soon to be) beautifully adorned temple standing in the midst of a renewed and righteous community.

Is 60:19–22. The intervention of Yahweh will be an earth-shaking transformation. Here the prophet speaks in the apocalyptic style, of a change in the order of nature where it has hitherto been most reliable—in the ordered movement of sun and moon. The imagery is apocalyptic; the content is eschatological. The continuity of this age and the age to come (the day of the Lord) is broken to such a degree in the prophet's vision that the word 'eschatological' is appropriate.

Is 60: 13 speaks of the new second temple. Read the account of laying its foundations, in Ezra 3: 10–13. How can the people of God best deal with the divergence of those who regret the passing of the past and those who rejoice in the coming of the future?

Is 61:1–7. The prophet speaks, unusually, in his own person. As 58 seems to issue from a day of fasting, and 60 from some covenant renewal liturgy, 61 may come from a jubilee year celebration. The jubilee was every fiftieth year, a year of release and amnesty for debtors and other prisoners laid down in Lev 25: 10.

As at one period the population of Israel freed their priests from worldly work and supported them to do the work of temple worship, so the general population of the world will free Israel for priestly service! A curious sub-ordination, possibly to be explained as rhetoric—a dramatic reversal of the existing state of affairs in which Israel was still a prey to invading, marauding gentile neighbours. This 'priestly' idea of priesthood was not the only one in the OT tradition. In earlier days, the passover was a feast presided over by fathers of families. Deuter-onomy speaks of the blessings that come from ordinary work in the world—in the fields. And (as was mentioned in the introduction to 56–66) the priesthood in post-exilic judaism gradually declined in importance as the teaching function of scribes and rabbis increased.

Is 61:8–11. The prophet speaks the words of Yahweh and

the Israelite responds with a prayer of thankfulness and confidence.

1. Examine the use Jesus made of 61:1–2, according to Luke (4:16–30).

2. What ideas of priesthood and ministry come over in this chapter? What are the elements of the tradition that ought to be emphasised today? And minimised, or discarded?

Is 62:1–9. The people are still expressing disappointment at the apparent non-fulfilment of 2-Isaiah's prophecies. Against a dark background of disillusion, 3-Isaiah continues to give his answers. In chapter 60 he seems to have answered the complaint that enemies were still harassing Israel; in 61, the charge that Israel was still suffering hardships; and now, in 62, the objection that God has not kept faith with Israel, but instead withdrawn into inactivity and 'silence' (64:12).

No such silence will the prophet keep. He will preach unceasingly for the restoration of the community, and he and his followers are busy reminding Yahweh that Israel is waiting for him (62:6). Yahweh's new initiative—the new covenant relationship, flowering into the married joy of Israel with her God—is at hand. Yahweh has promised.

Is 62:10–12. Here, 3-Isaiah uses the language of 2-Isaiah, but in a changed context. Now, it seems, the first returned exiles in Jerusalem are urged to prepare the way for the return of others still hesitating in Babylonia. They are urged to do this in terms of a liturgical procession into the city or the temple court, for worship. And these two ideas—the physical return of more exiles and public worship—are linked together by a third, conversion of the heart to holiness.

After all, Yahweh is faithful and the initiative is his: hence, Israel will be 'sought out'.

How do you see the difference between 2-Isaiah and 3-Isaiah? Is one utopian, and the other realistic? Or does one have full hope, and the other defective hope adulterated with discouragement?

Is 63:1–6. The theme of the rout of Israel's enemies (see 59:15–19; 62:8) is resumed, in a dialogue between Yahweh (though he is not explicitly named) and the prophet, speaking as a watchman guarding the walls. The Lord has come in person and carried out a violent revenging judgement on Israel's enemies. The year of salvation and release for some is the year of judgement for others (63:4). Edom was a people to the south of Judah, near the Dead Sea, and Bosrah was their city. The Edomites (whom Israel took to be the offspring of the rejected Esau, as they were offspring of the chosen Jacob) were foremost in raiding and ravaging Judah during the exile and the early days of reconstruction.

This passage is so discordant with most of Is 40–66 that some say it is an apocalyptic piece by someone other than 3-Isaiah, inserted here later (as the apocalyptic chapters 24–27 were inserted into 1-Isaiah).

Is 63:7–14. Here begins a prayer which continues till the end of chapter 64, perhaps a prayer with which Israel importuned Yahweh (62:6), or (and) a prayer spoken by some of those left in the ruins of Judah during the exile. There is a recital of God's saving acts, a word of trust in his choice of Israel, and a word to make her afflictions intelligible.

Is 63:15–19. The wretchedness of Israel's situation is apparent in a prayer of distress. The nation's founding

fathers, Abraham and Jacob, would not recognise Israel
now in her present abject misery. Lord, return! (63:18
may refer to the fall of Jerusalem to Babylon in 587, or to
some later Edomite invasion which interrupted the
reconstruction after 537.)

*Does 63:1–6 represent a tradition divergent from most of Is
40–66? Do you expect consistency in religious belief? If not,
how far can pluralism go without credibility evaporating?*

Is 64:1–12. This is the rest of the prayer, or psalm of
lamentation, which began at 63:7. It goes over ground
which is now familiar. Two particular points: (1) At
64:1—'rend the heavens and come down'—here is a
striking example of the biblical 'three-decker-universe'
cosmogony, which recurs at Mk 1:10 at the story of
Jesus's baptism. (2) At 64:8 (and 63:16) God is 'Father'
of Israel. God is very rarely called Father of Israel (never,
till post-exilic times) because so many of her gentile
neighbours expressed their relationship to their gods in
mythological terms of fatherhood and generation. Commonly, Israel called Yahweh her creator.

The final question put by the community to God
(64:12) is the question continually being asked in 3-
Isaiah's time, and the question he is continually attempt-
ing to answer.

*The biblical authors take as fact some things like the three-
storied universe which we now know are fancy, or 'mythology'.
How far should the 'demythologisation' of scripture be taken?*

Is 65:1–16. The editors seem to have intended 65 and 66
to stand where they do as Yahweh's reply to Israel's
lament and question in 63:7 and 64:12. (This pattern of
petition and response is familiar in the psalms.) To

Israel's question, 'wilt thou keep silent', Yahweh answers them that he has been yearning to get into touch with his people, but they turned their backs and busied themselves with idolatry, spiritualism, and unclean foods. So judgement impends, but (65:8) not for all. A prophet before the exile would probably have passed judgement on the nation as a whole (except perhaps for a faithful remnant) regarding the sins of some as implicating all. The 'disestablishment' of Israel in 587, and its modified status as more a 'gathered' people, make a difference. Now, there is a clear division (65:8–16) between sinners to be judged and faithful to be saved. And now that the adverse judgement is not on the nation as a whole but on a section of it—on certain individuals living side by side with other individuals—it cannot be executed (as in 587) through historical disaster affecting all alike. Judgement is transferred to some future date (eventually to a future life): the sins of the unrighteous are written before God, and he will repay (65:6).

Is 65:17–25. Here the wicked have dropped out of view, and we are back in the main stream of Is 40–66 with a prophecy of salvation for all. The existing state of things will be replaced by a new order, a rejuvenated creation, in which ideal terrestrial conditions will prevail. There will be health, long life, prosperity and freedom. Sorrow, strife, frustration and premature death will be absent. By allusion (65:25 and 11:6) this is the future kingdom of God brought by the messiah.

Scripture has two visions of the new creation. There is the apocalyptic 'new heaven and new earth', radically discontinuous with the present creation (Rev 21:1, 2 Pet 3:12–13). And there is 2-Isaiah's 'new thing'—Israel's release, return, and restoration—a strictly temporal and

terrestrial happening, though perhaps conceived in terms
of a return to the conditions of primeval paradise.

> *There is a christian prayer to the Holy Spirit (from the
> liturgy of Pentecost, drawing on Psalm 104:30):*
> > *Send forth thy Spirit, and they shall be created,
> > And thou shalt renew the face of the earth.*
> *How far this-worldly, and how far other-worldly—how far in
> time as we know it—is 3-Isaiah's picture of God's renewal?*

Is 66:1–24. This final chapter contains an unusually
large number of short separate units, of different dates
and probably by different authors; the themes are rather
widely divergent.

Is 66:1–2. The prophet Haggai and his school of thought
insisted that salvation was entirely conditional on the rebuilding of the temple and the resumption of sacrificial
worship. This passage is probably an assertion to the
contrary—that the word of God, and salvation, were
available, as throughout the exile, independently of the
temple.

Is 66:3–4. While this is obviously against idolatry in
general, the particular meaning is not very clear. It may
be saying that idolaters, even when carrying out sacrifices
which would be legitimate in temple worship, are still an
abomination to Yahweh.

Is 66:5. Reflects the cleavage in the community between
the faithful and the unfaithful.

Is 66:6–16. The temple (6) now seems to be built. 66:6
and 66:15–16, speaking of an almost physical coming of

the Lord, frame another salvation-prophecy for Jerusalem in terms of a miraculous birth without pains.

Is 66:17. An additional threat against idol-worshippers. 'The one in the midst' is apparently the leader in some ritual.

Is 66:18–24. Here, two of the themes of Is 40–66—the universalist and the nationalist—are stated together, and clash rather discordantly. It looks as if, after 3-Isaiah's time, later editors of differing schools of thought added appendices to the prophecies and fought to have the last word.

The universalistic theme is in 66:18, 19 and 21. A missionary movement will bring knowledge of God to the gentiles in farthest Spain, Somalia and Turkey. Gentiles will even join the priesthood and be leaders in the worship of Yahweh!

The particularist, nationalist theme is in 66:20 and 22–24. 66:20, practically a footnote to 18–19, explains that the missionary movement is really a movement to retrieve and bring back to Jerusalem the dispersed members of Israel. And 66:22–24 is an assurance to Israel of the continuance of her worship, coupled with a complementary assurance of the final destruction of her enemies, rebels against Yahweh.

It is important to know that below Jerusalem's south wall lay the valley of the Hinnom, the city's rubbish dump, where fire continually burnt dry refuse and worms unceasingly devoured the wet. We are left with a picture of the chosen faithful going out from the temple after their worship, looking over the wall, and viewing with satisfaction the bodies of the unrighteous consigned to a destruction outside the city as everlastingly terrible as the salvation wrought by temple worship within the city will be everlastingly sublime.

1. Does Is 40–66 present the temple as a sacred and holy place and see the rest of the world as secular, profane, unholy?

2. Read Is 66: 24 and Mk 9: 48 in conjunction. What light is thrown on the doctrine of hell?

3. How far is the language of Is 40–66 the language of prayer, psalm and poem, and how far the language of doctrine, dogma and creed?